Autobiography of Sir Walter Besant

Autobiography of Sir Walter Besant

Walter Besant

MINT EDITIONS

Autobiography of Sir Walter Besant was first published in 1902.

This edition published by Mint Editions 2021.

ISBN 9781513291062 | E-ISBN 9781513293912

Published by Mint Editions®

 MINT
EDITIONS

minteditionbooks.com

Publishing Director: Jennifer Newens
Design & Production: Rachel Lopez Metzger
Project Manager: Micaela Clark
Typesetting: Westchester Publishing Services

Contents

A Prefatory Note

*". . . It is hard to speak of him within measure when we consider
his devotion to the cause of authors, and the constant good service
rendered by him to their material interests. In this he was a valorous,
alert, persistent advocate, and it will not be denied by his opponents
that he was always urbane, his object being simply to establish a
system of fair dealing between the sagacious publishers of books and
the inexperienced, often heedless, producers. How unselfishly, with
how pure a generosity he gave his valuable time to the previously
neglected office of adviser to the more youthful of his profession, may
be estimated by a review of his memorable labours in other fields. They
were vast and toilsome, yet he never missed an occasion for acting as
the young author's voluntary friend in the least sentimental and most
sensible manner. He had no thought of trouble or personal loss where
the welfare of his fellow-workers was concerned. . ."*

—Mr. George Meredith, writing of Sir Walter Besant in
the *Author* of July, 1901

A n autobiography should be its own justification and its own
interpretation. There should be no room for a preface and no need
for any intermediary between the writer and the public to whom he has
designed to appeal. If it is necessary to add much to an autobiography,
the author is made to appear to have suppressed things that he should
have said; if any passages are deleted, the portrait of himself which
he proposed to draw is rendered incomplete. I have kept these things
before me, and in preparing Sir Walter Besant's autobiography for the
press have confined the modifications to the correction of obvious slips,
and to the addition of certain passages—mainly quotations from his
own works*—to which references were made in the manuscript. Only
a few words are called for, but the circumstances in which Sir Walter
Besant's autobiography is being published require a little explanation.
These circumstances account for the slight corrections that have been
made, as well as for the obvious incompleteness of his record in certain

---

* Messrs. Chatto and Windus, the publishers of Sir Walter Besant's novels, have kindly
given permission for the inclusion of these passages in the autobiography.

directions. It has been felt by his widow, by the executors of his will, and by his literary executor, that this, in justice to his memory, should be made clear to the reader.

Sir Walter Besant's autobiography was written for publication, and no one had any right to withhold the book from the public. Yet although Sir Walter Besant expressly meant his account of his life to be published, death overtook him before he had prepared it for press. Those who were familiar with the man and his literary methods know well what that means; they know that the autobiography is not presented in the form it would have appeared in had it undergone the minute revision to which all his written matter was subjected. His limpid style did not betray the fact that he was a rigorous critic of himself. In the eleventh chapter of the autobiography he explains to all whom it may interest his manner of writing a book. He compares it to the task of an engineer constructing a tunnel, drilling and mining, completing the work behind while thrusting the pick into the work ahead. This autobiography is to some extent an unfinished tunnel. Being an autobiography, the course of the work was clearly indicated to the author, who was able to dispense with a rough draft. But what he should include and what he should omit, what he should treat fully and what he should regard as episodes, had to be considered, and this was certainly not done by Besant in all places with his usual thorough care. If he had followed his invariable plan of composition, he would have made up his mind on many such points only when he came to the actual task of revising. This revision was wont to be done upon his manuscript roughly, and then very fully upon a type-written copy of that manuscript. The manuscript of the autobiography had not been type-written. The written manuscript was fully and freely corrected, and it may be taken for granted that the earlier portions of the work now appear much as they were intended to appear; but the later chapters would certainly have been amplified, and possibly modified in some directions. Such revision cannot be done now by anyone, however sure we may feel that it would have been done by him. If certain passages appear to readers to be unnecessarily sweeping, and especially if those who enjoyed a personal acquaintance with Besant find expressions of opinion in his posthumous memoir which hardly represent the man they knew, I would press that these points may be remembered: that he died leaving the manuscript in what he would have considered an unfinished state; that it was his express desire that it should be published; and that any attempt to modify his work either by addition or subtraction, however honest in its intention to make a more accurate picture, would amount to a dangerous tampering with the original.

The autobiography does Besant scant justice, but, in noting the deficiencies, I do so with no completely unnecessary eulogy, and no equally unnecessary apology. Nor do I attempt to point out places where I believe the author would have made alterations. The revision might have taken the form of some modification of words, or the addition of other matter which would have altered the proportions of the work, and no one can guess which change, if any, would have been made. But it is permissible to say a few prefatory words to guard against false impressions, the creation of which would certainly not have been risked had Besant revised his manuscript as a whole.

Firstly, then, although Sir Walter Besant with much directness, and several times, inveighs against the evangelical tenets which prevailed in his youth, and although he enunciates at the end of his autobiography his religious creed with complete clearness, there is no real connection between his creed and his dislike of evangelical teaching. From a religious point of view his dislike was rather to ritualism. His hatred—for no other word can be used—of the evangelical teaching of his youth was an expression of his delight in life, and had nothing to do with his sacred convictions. He saw the beauty of holiness, but he loathed the doctrine that it was wrong to be happy in this world—the idea that heaven was propitiated by the earthly misery of those who sought to be good. He perceived the stupid, inconsistency and illogicality of those who held that the small section who did as they did would be saved whatever their failings, while all who differed from them about such a minor ethical point as, say, the propriety of play-going, must be irretrievably damned, whatever their virtues. "If a person," says Overton in *The English Church of the Nineteenth Century* with regard to the evangelical school, "was enjoying a well-spread feast at Clapham, with all the charms of the conversation of Wilberforce or Milner—which to many people would be infinitely more entertaining than most of the so-called entertainments provided by 'the world'—he was doing right, and was, so far as outward surroundings went, on the way to heaven. But if he was reading one of Miss Austen's novels, or at a dance, or a concert, or at a card-table (not necessarily gambling), or seeing one of Goldsmith's delightful plays acted, he was doing wrong, and, so far as outward surroundings, was in plain words on the way to hell." Besant was born and bred in touch with these views, and imbibed a horror of their cruelty.

And if an intense dislike of seeing people wantonly made unhappy set him against the tenets of the party in the English Church with which he should have had most affinity, so an equally intense dislike of the mystical set him against ritualism. Sir Walter Besant was a clear-headed man who delighted in thinking out mental and social problems for himself, and detested anything that savoured of the incomprehensible. In more than one of his novels an important situation is the exposure of the vain pretension of one of the characters to extraordinary powers—powers of supernatural achievement, powers of discrimination or criticism of higher and more delicate character than those granted to ordinary mortals. He was ready to allow that we now see only through a glass darkly; but he was not ready to allow that any form of ordination would make one man see further than another, nor to believe that ceremonial might help insight by helping faith. Feeling deeply as he did the mystery of immortality, he resented any assumption on the part of a class of ability to see further into the mystery than other persons. Sir Walter Besant was, it must always be remembered, a scholar—and so successful a scholar that although in his modest record of his achievements he makes light of what he did as a young man, it is quite clear that he was from childhood an intellectual leader. His natural place was at the head. To his intellectual equals, and especially to men of leading in different departments of learning, he was always willing to defer; but to a priesthood basing their right to interpret the Word of God on other than intellectual grounds he could not bring himself to listen. To some this attitude will seem intolerant, and to some it will seem sensible; but to all who knew Sir Walter Besant it will seem the only possible one for him. Perhaps he may appear to speak against priestly authority—or priestly interposition, as he regarded it—with a little acerbity, but such an element was so completely foreign to his sweet and genial nature that we may be sure that its appearance is accidental, and would have been removed if the writer had been spared to think over his words.

In another place in his autobiography Sir Walter Besant's words are more insistent than they need have been to give a fair representation of his feelings. I refer to his repeated allusions to the shortcomings of a certain class of literary critic. Here again, I am convinced, the appearance of acerbity is out of proportion to the real state of his sentiments. He was not always fairly reviewed, and in particular his antiquarian learning and faithful reproduction, at whatever cost of time or trouble, of local colour often had scant justice done to them. But he will have given a wrong impression of himself—a completely wrong and unworthy impression—if he leads his readers to believe that his attitude towards critics was inspired by wounds to his own literary vanity. To begin with, Besant received always sufficient hearty support in the best quarters to make him feel that it did not hurt him to be belittled here and there; and secondly, he was the least vain of men. No. Besant was hurt and annoyed with a certain class of critics because, as he conceived their duty, they had no proper qualifications to perform it. They were not scholars, and had no business to attempt to stand between the public and the writer; they had no literary or practical experience either to enable them to tell the author what was good, bad, and indifferent in his books, or to help the reader to choose his mental food aright. He scented in the sayings of these ill-equipped judges the savour of charlatanism that always offended him—their pretensions annoyed him as those of the ritualist annoyed him. He believed, and probably more than occasionally with some justice, that the airs of omniscience concealed depths of ignorance; while perhaps he hardly recognised that it is much easier now than it was in his own young days to get a working knowledge of an author without deep reading. In the 'fifties and 'sixties, if a man wanted to know about—for example—Rabelais or Balzac, he would have to read their works. And he would have to read them all, if he had no well-informed friend to guide him in making a selection; otherwise he could come to no judgment that would be worth quoting, or that he would dare to depend upon. Today, thanks to Besant, among other men of letters, there are monographs and exact treatises which deal with all accepted classics, so that it is possible for the critic to speak and write as though his reading had been vastly wider than is the case, and at the same time to be fairly correct. I think Besant hardly realised this fact when he put down the men, who paraded an intimate knowledge where a nodding acquaintance was all that they possessed, as necessarily wrong in what they said.

In his younger days the acquisition of exact knowledge was harder, and perhaps, therefore, more prized. It must be remembered that Sir Walter Besant's particular friends at college were all men of learning. Christ's College, Cambridge, during his time was a particularly brilliant establishment. Besant belonged to the reading set, and was brought up in a school of hard work. His knowledge was fought for, and recalling the difficulty that he had experienced in obtaining it, he found it hard to realise that nowadays knowledge is easier to come by. Again, he was impatient of facile criticism because he had an immense opinion of the dignity of letters, and a great pride, as a novelist, in the part that novels had played in the education and development of peoples. He could not believe that it was either sound policy on the part of an editor, or fair play towards a writer, to hand good work by responsible men over to a glib critic, to whom only a few lines could be allotted in which, upon imperfect information, he must express a summary judgment. In behalf both of letters and of fiction he protested against the custom, without perhaps quite appreciating the editorial position in the matter. However, I have no intention of trying to explain away what he has said; I write only to make it clear that his views are expressed in the autobiography in a disproportionate manner. To read him one would think that the iniquity of critics was a subject upon which he was constantly brooding; as a matter of fact, it was a subject in which he took no deeper interest than scores of literary men, while it must be again repeated that what interest he took was in no sense personal. He was jealous for the position and privileges of authors as a whole, and the stress that is laid upon the shortcomings of some of their professional appraisers is due to this. It would not have been so noticeable if the autobiography had been a complete and rounded story. It is not. It is an exposition of the novelist's life, showing how good a life it is when conscientious work meets with success. Besant elaborated the record of those parts of his life which he conceived to have had a particular influence upon his choice of a career, and upon the position to which he attained in literature. For the rest his tale is made up of somewhat disconnected notes, which serve to show the depth as well as the multiplicity of his interests, but which have not been written by him with strict regard to proportion. It is possible that, if he had lived to complete and revise his work, many of the gaps would have been filled up; but even so, the later chapters would not have contained, I think, the minute personal details of the earlier—those which describe the evolution of the novelist, the character that he meant to portray.

If it had been felt that any critical estimate of Sir Walter Besant's work would form a fitting introduction to his autobiography, the task would have been committed to someone of his own literary position and weight; and that a critic of this quality may soon speak with no uncertain voice upon the matter I hope sincerely. But it is clear from his own words that he would have preferred that no summing up of his imaginative work should be given hastily. It was a part of his high conception of the novelist's duties to dislike all attempts at placing novelists above or below one another in some arbitrary hierarchy, and all labelling of them as belonging to this or that school of thought. "It is sufficient," he would have said for himself, "to read my books—I desire to be judged by them"; while he would not have considered a novelist to have wholly succeeded in his craft if his work required much interpretation, or if many reasons had to be found for its want of popularity. He was aware of the pellucid nature of his productions, he was aware how little they required the assistance of the critic, and how entirely the explanation of the point of view was superfluous. Straightforward characters, set in an accurate environment, often subtly and very often delicately drawn, but about whose significance there never could be a shadow of doubt, tell their own stories in his pages, and while revealing their characteristics complete the narrative. What need of explanation? Well, only this. Sir Walter Besant by practice—painstaking practice, as he informs us—learned to use so facile a pen that his limpid prose, together with his rigorous habits of emendation, resulted in a page that was extremely easy to read, and the pains which it might have cost to write were never really appreciated. Again, the conscientious care with which all his pictures of men and manners were set in a suitable frame, escaped the notice of his critics, because his historical information was utilised without parade. Passages proving a really wonderful familiarity with eighteenth-century habits were often regarded as so much padding to a pretty tale, because his smooth methods made his performance seem obvious. If the tale had been less pretty, more attention would have been paid to the *mise-en-scène*; the treasures of accurate knowledge, lovingly and laboriously acquired, would have been better appreciated if they had been more forced upon the attention. But that is exactly the sort of thing that Besant would never wittingly provide for. He loved his stories, and to exalt his own learning by laying disproportionate stress upon some minor incident, and by so doing to imperil the symmetry or verisimilitude of his work, would have been abhorrent to him. I trust that some sound judge, a man with learning to appreciate Besant's scholarly equipment, and with sympathy for the difficulties which the author created for himself by the strict limitations within which he was resolved to abide, will in the near future give us an authoritative note upon Sir Walter Besant's fiction.

Sir Walter Besant never lived to complete the work which would have established him at once and forever in the public eye as a historian and antiquary—I mean the *Survey of London*. In the fourteenth chapter of the autobiography, wherein he describes the scope of the vast scheme that he had undertaken, he speaks of the *Survey of London* as no inconsiderable part of his life-work. As a matter of fact, the task that he laid upon himself was enormous. He proposed with his own pen to write the history of London from the earliest times to the end of the nineteenth century, taking into account the chief historical events in their political and historical bearing. Special sections of the work—scientific education in London, the story of the London stage, the work and position of the Metropolitan hospitals, are three such sections that occur to my mind at once—he proposed to delegate to selected writers; but their contributions would have been welded by him, according to his design, into a symmetrical whole. He did not live to accomplish the task; but he made such headway with it that the whole of the history from his own hand is finished in manuscript, and one volume is in type. He commenced his labours by arranging for perambulations of the whole city in imitation of Strype's "circuit-walk taken for diversion four or five miles round about," and as it is six years since these perambulations were done, it follows that today they are in a sense out of date. I say in a sense, for in another sense a history of London is never out of date, just as it can never be up to date. No history of London can do more than mark a stage, from which point other writers will take up the tale. The perambulations in Besant's *Survey* are not true of 1901; but if they had been true of 1901 they would not have been true of 1902. To many it will seem fortunate that his perambulations were made a little before the pulling down of ancient buildings that has been necessitated by certain of the recent and comprehensive improvement schemes. They gain thereby in interest for present readers; while the only drawback is that the historian of the future will have to build upon Besant's structure, beginning at 1897, instead of at the more obvious date of 1901. The year 1901, which saw the commencement of the new century and the death of the Great Queen whose reign forms such a distinct and splendid epoch in our national development, was felt by Sir Walter Besant to be the ideal date up to which to bring his history, but the glory and pleasure of doing this have been denied him. He made however sufficient progress to show how capable he would have been to carry out his colossal design. Let me quote a small passage taken quite at random from the perambulations to show what kind of a book Besant had planned. They are the first sentences in the perambulation of Fulham, the section of the manuscript dealing with Fulham being by the kindness of Messrs. A. & C. Black under my hand:—

"If we enter Fulham at the extreme north-east corner, the point where the Hammersmith Road crosses the District Railway between the Addison Road and West Brompton stations, we find ourselves in the ward numbered one on the Vestry map and known as Baron's Court. When Faulkner wrote his history of Fulham (1813) this was still a country district, containing only a few scattered houses, along the North End Road. Avonmore Road runs south from the boundary, and in it there is a sorting office of the Post Office. William Street is parallel to it, and has board schools on either side. That on the west was built in 1874, and subsequently added to, that on the east in 1886. Further south, William Street becomes Lisgar Terrace. The North End Road, which is a little further westward, begins at the Hammersmith Road, and for part of its course runs due north and south. In it stands a chapel of the United Methodist Free Church. It is singularly devoid of any pretension to beauty, being a square structure of dingy brick. Further south, just before the North End Road curves round to meet Edith Road, are two old houses on the left hand side. They are known as 'The Grange,' and were formerly one building. The southern half is of red brick, surrounded by a high wall, and has a gateway, with tall red brick pillars, surmounted by stone balls. Beyond this we catch a glimpse of a picturesque stable with creepers covering it. Over the wall hangs an acacia tree, and on the top right-hand corner of the house, just above a railed balcony, is an old sundial. The house is now the residence of Sir Edward Burne Jones. Its fellow adjoining has been painted a light stone colour, but shares in the glamour of old age. It is in the style of William III, and in a print published in *Richardson's Correspondence*, 1804, the house is shown divided into two, as at present. The red brick half was that occupied by the novelist, who lived here until 1755, when he moved to Parsons Green. Faulkner mentions it as having been 'lately altered and now occupied as two houses,' 1813. A little further south Edith Road branches off to the west. At the time of the 1860 edition of Crofton Croker's *Walk from London to Fulham*, it was to be 'let on building lease.' It is now a street of well-built occupied houses. In it Croker says 'once stood the house of Cipriani,' the designer. But there seems to be some doubt as to the exact site of Cipriani's house, for in Thome's *Environs of London* it is stated, 'In the lane opposite to Edith Road lived Cipriani.' Cipriani lived in England from 1755 to 1785, and his works were largely engraved by Bartolozzi, who also had a house at North End, and who is mentioned at some length by Faulkner."

Can we not picture the delight of the antiquarian, the historian, the romancer of the future in the possession of a book containing such information? And it was Besant's design to treat all London in the same way. The perambulation of Fulham goes on to give brief descriptions of such various things as the Queen's Club grounds, the Earl's Court Exhibition, Hurlingham, and Norman (or Normand) House; while considerable space is devoted, of course, to Fulham Palace and Fulham Parish Church. Strype's circuit-walk about Fulham occupies three columns of the well-known edition, and gives merely an account of the bishop's palace and the church and its monuments. Besant's perambulation of Fulham is over twenty times as long, and has records of all sorts of buildings and institutions, Fulham having grown, during the interval between the walks of the two chroniclers, from a beautiful little village to a busy and thickly populated quarter of the world's capital. The same enormous expansion of material had to be dealt with at every point of the compass; but Besant faced the tremendous difficulties with resolution. Well may he say in his autobiography that he considers his literary work in regard to London no inconsiderable part of his life's labours. For a less indefatigable man, what he managed to accomplish of the *Survey* would have sufficed for a lifetime of effort; and all who have regard for Besant's memory look forward to hearing that arrangements have been made for completing his great design.

A quality of Sir Walter Besant's autobiography must be touched upon—its modesty. It will only be touched upon, for to thrust praise upon one who shrank so from praise is somewhat of an outrage. The modesty in his autobiography is a fault that he would never have corrected, and throughout his record of his life he studiously underrates himself, hardly at anytime assuming credit for aught but industry. He regards a first-class scholastic career as creditable; his success at Mauritius is barely alluded to, only peeping out in the chance admission that the rectorship of the College was offered to him as the result of a dispute with his chief; his account of his share in the collaboration with James Rice is pointedly advantageous to Rice; his gratitude for the place that he won in literature is untinctured by a trace of vanity or jealousy; he forgets to mention his knighthood, and is silent upon that much coveted honour, election to the Athenæum Club under Rule II as "a person who has attained to a distinguished eminence in literature"; on his own labours of love in behalf of the Society of Authors he has practically nothing to say.

He gives the story of this Society, but leaves out as far as possible his personal share in that story. The self-sacrifice and devotion that he displayed in the conduct of the affairs of "our beloved Society," as he called the association in one of his addresses, would certainly have been made themes for lengthy notice in any life of Besant undertaken by another writer, and it is right to supplement his autobiography with a few words in this connection. For his attitude towards publisher and author was persistently misrepresented or misunderstood. He was generally accused of a sweeping hatred of publishers, and a short-sighted if generous desire to encourage incompetent writers. The accusations were founded on ignorance. His real attitude was this: having asserted that ordinary business routine, either carried out personally or by an accredited agent, cannot possibly be opposed to the production of matter of the first artistic excellence, he set to work to make clear the principles which should underlie the commercial relations of the author and the publisher. The literary merits of a particular author, the crystal probity of a particular publisher, had nothing to do with the case.

When the earliest business done by the Society of Authors made it clear that the publishing world—like every other trade and profession—contained a few black sheep, Besant declared that customs which allowed them a chance of making a livelihood ought to be discontinued by all publishers. It is difficult to believe that any right-minded judgment could consider such a view to be dictated either by wholesale and sweeping hatred of all publishers, or by a wish to make the path of the incompetent writer smoother. Sir Walter Besant was chairman of the Society of Authors on three separate occasions, his last tenure of office lasting from 1887 to 1892. Until the day of his death the affairs of the Society formed an integral part of his life, and while he was chairman the amount of time that he cheerfully spent upon its business is well-nigh incredible. During four years he went three or four days in the week to the office of the Society, prepared to discuss every imaginable point of difficulty. Nothing was too large for him to go through with, nothing was too small for him to attend to that bore upon the profession of letters. He became accessible to scores of persons who wasted his valuable time simply that he might not lose a chance of hearing a case where he could do good. And he took no credit for the enormous sacrifice of himself and the unceasing call upon his thoughts; on the contrary, if an opportunity occurred, he gave other people the praise.

Mr. Anthony Hope, speaking for the Committee of the Society of Authors, has thus expressed their views:—

"Faith, zeal, courage, self-devotion—these were the great qualities which he brought to his chosen work—the work of developing in men of letters a sense of their brotherhood, of the dignity of their profession, of the duty of maintaining steadfastly its independence and its rights." What he warred against was, in his own words, 'the feeling, ridiculous, senseless, and baseless, that it is beneath the dignity of an author to manage his business affairs as a man of business should, with the same regard for equity in his agreement, the same resolution to know what is meant by both sides of an agreement, and the same jealousy as to assigning the administration of his property.' Against the old bad way—the hand-to-mouth existence, indolence and ignorance parading as the superiority of genius, a slipshod negligence that ended in recrimination and wranglings, he set his own face and armed his comrades, for it was to his comrades in the first instance that his message spoke. Their fate was in their own hands; it was in their power to make justice, knowledge, and common sense prevail in their business arrangements. . . He said, 'I can at least plead that I have always placed the cause before any other consideration.' All our members know one sense in which this was so abundantly true. He placed it before his ease and his leisure; for its sake he endured violent

WALTER BESANT

attack, supercilious comment, ill-informed criticism; for it he suffered himself to be represented by many as false to the very thing he loved best of all—the true and highest interests of literature."

To this fine tribute to Besant's unselfish zeal in behalf of his craft, no one can desire to add a word; no one can take a word away from it without detracting from its accuracy.

If I repeat myself it is because the purpose of this prefatory note is to make clear the reason of certain limitations in the autobiography which follows. Sir Walter Besant has only designed to describe a working novelist's career; he expressly says that he is not making confessions, while he is almost silent upon his peaceful and happy private life. The manuscript which he left behind him was written in the last year of his life, when his health had begun to fail; and, even now that the passages which he referred to definitely as requiring insertion have been added, the work is not as he would have let it go forth. He never revised the manuscript as a whole, an important fact, because it was his habit to make considerable corrections in all his written work. Yet it is certain that he intended his autobiography to be published. For my own part, though I am sure that he would have improved the autobiography in certain directions if he could have followed the promptings of second thoughts, I am equally sure that the work as it stands must have a useful, nay a noble influence. A scholar who was never a pedant, a beautiful dreamer who was a practical teacher, a modest and sincere man speaks in its pages, and teaches with conviction a brave scheme of life.

S. Squire Sprigge
United University Club

I

Child and Boy

One's birth, as to period, place, social position, connections and education, should be determined by every man for himself before the event in accordance with the career, or the kind of work, destined for him by the Gods. I am supposing that he has the choice offered him, together with an outline of the future—not a future of fate laid down with Calvinistic rigour, but a future of possibility. And as time, past or future, does not exist in the other world, I am supposing that a man can be born in any age that he pleases. For many reasons I myself, though I speedily forgot the circumstances attendant on the choice, decided—quite rightly, I believe—that the nineteenth century, so far as I could judge—not being able to foretell the twentieth or following centuries—would be the most favourable time for a person like myself. "You," said my guardian angel, "are to be endowed with certain powers of imagination which you will do well to cultivate; you will have a tolerably good memory, which you will also cultivate, if you are wise; in good hands you might become a scholar, a divine, a preacher, a journalist, a novelist, or a historian. There will be limits, of course, to your powers. I fear that to you will not be granted the supreme gift of the foremost rank. But you will do what you can. How and where and when will you please to be born?"

A difficult choice. If a man is to be a statesman, he should be born in such a station as would enable him to take a place in the front at anytime, with the feeling that command and leadership belong to him; if a soldier, then he should be of a family connected with the Services, and not wholly without property. If a man is to become a clergyman, good breeding, good manners, and a public school education are invaluable. If a lawyer, or a physician, or any other profession, easy manners which come from good breeding are always a help. If on the other hand a man is destined to be a writer of the kind which demands imagination, sympathy, observation, then he should ask to be born neither in the lowest ruck nor in the upper levels. For in the former case the manners and the standards of the people would become part and parcel of himself, so that he would be unable to separate himself from them, or to describe them, or to understand them; while in the latter case he would have no chance of observing or knowing how those people live for whom getting their livelihood is the first and most important consideration. For such a writer the most favourable position to be born in is that of the so-called middle class, where one is not so far above the mass as not to know or to understand something of their thoughts and standards, of their manners, their customs and their convictions: and where one is yet so far removed as not to be led or guided by them, or to be unable to get outside their prejudices. For much the same reason one would not choose to be born in London, which is too vast; in London a child of the middle class grows up in a suburb, where he lives among respectable folk, and gets no knowledge either of higher society or lower. There have been, it is true, many children of London who have achieved greatness. Not to speak of Chaucer and Milton, Ben Jonson and Pope, there have been such writers as Charles Lamb and Hood; while Dickens and Thackeray also were practically Londoners, but in the days before suburban dullness. On the whole, a place outside London would seem preferable; that place not to be a quiet village, but a busy town, with its own distinctive character and its own distinctive people.

These arguments, in my theory of free and antenatal selection, prevailed, and I was allowed a seaport of the first rank as the place of birth; the second quarter of the nineteenth century as the time of birth; and the middle class for the social rank from which to start. In such a rank one begins by looking around and below, but not, as a rule, above.

I have no doubt in my own mind that it was also by choice that I became one of a large household, so that the rough and tumble of boys and girls together might knock out something of selfishness and something of conceit; a family where there was not too much money, and where economy was practised—yet without privation—in everything; and where one understood from the outset that for success, if success was desired—it is not every boy who is ambitious—there would have to be hard work. And I am equally certain of the benevolence of the guardian angel when I consider that, as regards work among books, I was born of an industrious turn of mind. It was, again, a most wholesome discipline to learn from childhood that whatever is wanted must be earned. It has been my lot to live among those who have succeeded by their own abilities and hard work, and I find, as a general rule, that the sons of such men have never learned this wholesome discipline, but have grown up in the belief that fortune's choicest gifts drop into the laps of those who sit and sleep in the sunshine and wait.

I was born, then, on the evening of Sunday, August the 14th, in the year 1836, now sixty-three years ago, the place being that known as St. George's Square, Portsea, a broad, open place of irregular shape lying on the east of the Common Hard, and containing a curious, sprawling barn of a church belonging to the time of George the Second. More about this Church presently. The number of the house where I saw the light was, I believe, three. I was the fifth child and the third son of a family of ten, of whom nine grew up, and at this moment, January 1900, seven survive.

Great changes have taken place in my native town since my early recollections. It was, in my boyhood, a strangely picturesque place in its own way. There was no other town in England at all like Portsmouth. It then consisted of three divisions: the old Town of Portsmouth; the eighteenth century Town of Portsea; and the Quarter called Point. The suburbs of Landport and Southsea were already growing—indeed, Dickens was born at Landport in the year 1812—but they were small places. The former contained a dozen streets, chiefly of a humble character, with a crescent of handsome villas standing in their own gardens; the latter contained one line of terraces, with a main street and two or three narrow lanes. The terraces were occupied by retired Service people and lodging house keepers—Southsea, from the beginning, was always a place for Service people.

There are no ancient buildings at all in Portsea, which is an eighteenth century town, or in the suburbs, but there are a few in Portsmouth. The Domus Dei, the mediaeval Hospital, has been converted into the Garrison Chapel; here Charles II married Catherine of Braganza. The old church of St. Thomas, with its ship for a weathercock, I always regarded with veneration, but I believe that only the chancel and the transepts are ancient. There is a square stone tower at the end of the High Street, with a gilt bust of Charles I, who landed here on his return—without the Infanta—from Spain. There were a few wooden houses in Portsmouth, and in my boyhood a large number of low, somewhat picturesque gabled houses belonging to the time when no dwellings were allowed to be higher than the town walls. One of them, unless I mistake, still survives.

The High Street, however, possessed the charm of a certain antiquity. The town hall, the house where the Duke of Buckingham was murdered, the quaint little Unitarian chapel, the "George" and "Fountain" inns, the red brick houses, and an air of quiet and dignity, not disturbed by recent traffic, made the street impressive. But the glory and pride of the town were its walls. There were two lines of fortification, that of Portsmouth and that of Portsea. One the other side of the harbour was a third line, the walls of Gosport. These walls were constructed on the well known system with a scarp, counterscarp, advanced works, a moat, gates and bridges, and bastions commanding the walls in flank and planted with cannon. A broad walk ran along the top of the walls, with a parapet from which the defender would fire over the sloping earthwork breast high. Trees were planted along the broad walks; upon every bastion there was a meadow with a grassy down slope; and at intervals there were stone watch towers. Between the walls of Portsea and those of Portsmouth was a broad sheet of water, called the Mill dam, which rose and fell with every tide—an artificial lake constructed with an eye to the fortifications. It had a causeway running across it and an island in the middle of it. The island contained a bastion and a small house, in which resided a sergeant and his family. This island, to live on which seemed to me the height of happiness, communicated with the causeway by means of an iron bridge. The walls, with the meadows before the bastion, the moat, the counterscarp, the advanced works and the Mill dam occupied a very considerable space. Outside the whole a clear area was kept on which no houses were permitted to be built. The suburbs of Portsmouth, therefore, were unconnected with the town; they lay beyond this clear space. The walls were the playground, the park, the breathing place for the children and the boulevard for the people. Old and young walked on the walls. Nursemaids took the children every fine day to the walls. They were quite safe, for if a child rolled down the sloping face its fall was over grass and into grass, and no harm was done. The little boys brought hoops, and ran them round the walls. They clambered about the bastions, and peered into the mouths of the cannon, and sat upon the gun carriages, and crept out fearfully through the embrasures, and, looking over into the moat below, played at seeing the enemy beyond; or they ran down the grassy slopes to the meadows, which in spring were spread with a golden carpet of buttercups. These excursions were illegal. There was a special police for the walls; it consisted of three or four men, reported to be of short temper, who carried canes, with which they "warmed" boys caught in the meadows or on the slopes. These guardians were called "Johnnies," and I always regarded them as unfortunate men of a misanthropic turn whose occupation, to catch and "warm" boys, was also their pleasure. But as regards ourselves, I think that measures of conciliation had been adopted, because we seem to have run about everywhere, on the slopes or over the meadows, or even in the embrasures, unmolested.

One of the bastions was our especial delight. It was the last on the side of the harbour; it was more secluded than the others, being farther from the town, and few children found their way to it. They called it the Queen's Bastion. I have described the place in one of my novels—that called *By Celia's Arbour*. It is not doing an injustice to the memory of my collaborateur, the late James Rice, who was not a Portsmouth man and had never seen the place, to claim that part of the story which belongs to the town as my own. Let me therefore quote a little from that book:—

"Our playground was a quiet place, especially at our end, where the town children, to whom the ramparts elsewhere were the chief place of recreation, seldom resorted. There were earthworks planted with trees and grass, and the meadows beneath were bright with buttercups and daisies. We were privileged children; we might run up and down the slopes or on the ramparts, or through the embrasures, or even clamber about the outer scarp down to the very edge of the moat, without rebuke from the 'Johnnies,' the official guardians of the walls, who went about all day armed with canes to keep boys from tearing down the earthworks. It was this privilege, as well as the general convenience of the place for children to play in, which took us nearly everyday to the Queen's Bastion. There never was a more delightful retreat. In summer the trees afforded shade, and in winter the rampart gave shelter. You were in a solitude almost unbroken, close to a great centre of life and busy work; you looked out upon the world beyond, where there were fields, gardens, and trees; there was our own round corner, with the stately elms above us; the banks of grass, all sorts of grass, as one finds where there is no cultivation, trembling grass, foxtail grass, and that soft, bushy grass for which we had no name; there was the gun mounted on its high carriage, gazing out upon the harbour, a one-eyed Polyphemus longing for human food.

"We (Leonard, Celia, and Ladislas Pulaski, who tells the story) were standing, as I said, in the north-west corner of the Queen's Bastion, the spot where the grass was longest and greenest, the wild convolvulus most abundant, and where the noblest of the great elms which stood upon the ramparts—'to catch the enemy's shells,' said Leonard—threw out a gracious arm laden with leafy foliage to give a shade. We called the place Celia's Arbour.

"If you looked out over the parapet, you saw before you the

whole of the most magnificent harbour in the world; and if you looked through the embrasure of the wall, you had a splendid framed picture—water for foreground, old ruined castle in middle distance, blue hill beyond, and above blue sky.

"We were all three silent, because it was Leonard's last evening with us. He was going away, our companion and brother, and we were there to bid him God speed.

"It was after eight; suddenly the sun, which a moment before was a great disc of burnished gold, sank below the thin line of land between sky and sea.

"Then the evening gun from the Duke of York's Bastion proclaimed the death of another day with a loud report, which made the branches in the trees above us to shake and tremble. And from the barracks in the town; from the Harbour Admiral's flagship; from the Port Admiral's flagship; from the flagship of the Admiral in command of the Mediterranean Fleet, then in harbour; from the tower of the old church, there came such a firing of muskets, such a beating of drums, playing of fifes, ringing of bells, and sounding of trumpets, that you would have thought the sun was setting once for all, and receiving his farewell salute from a world he was leaving forever to roll about in darkness.

"The evening gun and the *tintamarre* that followed roused us all three, and we involuntarily turned to look across the parapet. Beyond that was the moat, and beyond the moat was a ravelin, and beyond the ravelin the sea-wall; beyond the wall a smooth and placid lake, for it was high tide, four miles long, and a couple of miles wide, in which the splendour of the west was reflected so that it looked like a furnace of molten metal. At low tide it would have been a great flat level of black mud, unlovely even with an evening sky upon it, intersected with creeks and streams which, I suppose, were kept full of water by the drainage of the mud-banks.

"At the end of the harbour stood the old ruined castle, on the very margin and verge of the water. The walls were reflected in the calm bosom of the lagoon; the water-gate opened out upon the wavelets of the lapping tide; behind rose the great donjon, square, grey, and massive; in the tourney-yard stood the old church, and we needed no telling to make us think of the walls behind, four feet broad, rugged and worn by the tooth of Time, thickly blossoming with gilly-flowers, clutched and held on all sides by the tight embrace of the ivy. There had been rain in the afternoon, so that the air was clear and transparent, and you could see every stone in the grand old keep, every dentation of the wall.

"Behind the castle lay the low curved line of a long hill, green and grassy, which made a background to the harbour and the old fortress. It stretched for six miles, this hill, and might have been monotonous but for the chalk quarries which studded its side with frequent intervals of white. Farther on, to the west, there lay a village, buried in a great clump of trees, so that you could see nothing but the tower of a church and the occasional smoke of a chimney. The village was so far off that it seemed like some outlying fort, an advance work of civilisation, an outpost such as those which the Roman conquerors have left in the desert. When your eye left the village among the trees and travelled southwards, you could see very little of land on the other side by reason of the ships which intervened—ships of every age, of every class, of every colour, of every build; frigates, three-deckers, brigs, schooners, cutters, launches, gunboats, paddle-wheel steamers, screw steamers, hulks so old as to be almost shapeless—they were lying ranged in line, or they w6re moored separately; some in the full flood of the waning sunset, some in shadow, one behind the other, making deep blacknesses in the golden water. There was not much life at this late hour in the harbour. Here and there a boat pulled by two or three lads from the town; here and there a great ship's gig, moving heavily through the water, pulled by a crew of sailors, rowing with their slow and measured stroke, and the little middy sitting in the stern; or perhaps a wherry coming down from Fareham Creek. But mostly the harbour was silent, the bustle at the lower end having ceased with the sunset."

Later on it was a practice to go once a year with a small party to Porchester. The visit was timed for the holiday of a certain D. A——, a civil servant of some department in London. He took his holiday in July or August, and used to join our little excursion, which he made merry by a thousand jokes and quips and quirks. He was always in good spirits and always ready with a laugh. We got to Porchester by boat, if the tide served; if not, by rail part of the way and walking the rest. No one can ever be tired of Porchester. There are the old Roman walls, with their hollow bastions. One side faces the harbour, the *magnus portus*, with a water gate; on the other side is a moat of Plantagenet addition. In one corner is a long narrow church with Saxon details, but rebuilt by the Normans; in its churchyard lie not only the bones of men-at-arms from the garrison and the rude forefathers of the hamlet, but also those of hundreds of French prisoners kept here during the long war of 1795–1815. A whole regiment of West Indian negroes—prisoners of war—died in one winter, and were buried in this churchyard. In another corner is a Norman castle, with its tall keep and its inner bastion. On our annual visit we began by climbing to the roof of the keep and by walking round the walls and looking into the chambers; this done, we had tea in one of the houses outside the walls. There was no tea like the Porchester tea; no bread like that of this happy village; no butter, no cake, no shrimps comparable with theirs. After tea we walked home—seven miles. Presently the sun went down: then the tall trees stood up against the sky like giants with long arms threatening; the air became mysterious, charged with sounds the meaning of which we could not catch; there were muffled notes of birds; silly cockchafers buzzed about and flew in our faces. The party became silent, even D. A—— ceased to make jokes; and the long mysterious march in the summer twilight lingers in my memory for the solemn joy, the sense of mystery, the feeling of the life invisible which fell upon one at least of that small company.

My father, who was born in the year 1800, in the first month of the last year of the 18th century, could remember very well the French prisoners at Porchester. As a boy he would take a boat up the harbour and go to the castle to see the prisoners. He spoke of their vivacity, their little industries—they made all kinds of ingenious things—and their friendliness with the boys, who laughed at their lingo and tried to make them understand English. Somewhere about the year 1883 or so, I wrote a story called *The Holy Rose*, in which I laid the scene partly in the village and castle of Porchester:—

"The village of Porchester is a place of great antiquity, but it is little, and except for its old Castle of no account. Its houses are all contained in a single street, beginning at the Castle-gate and ending long before you reach the Portsmouth and Fareham road, which is only a quarter of a mile from the Castle. Most of them are mere cottages, with thatched or red-tiled roofs, but they are not mean or squalid cottages; the folk are well-to-do, though humble, and every house in the village, small or great, is covered all over, back and front, with climbing roses. The roses cluster over the porches, they climb over the red tiles, they peep into the latticed windows, they cover and almost hide the chimney. In the summer months the air is heavy with their perfume; every cottage is a bower of roses; the flowers linger sometimes far into the autumn, and come again with the first warm days of June. Nowhere in the country, I am sure, though I have seen a few other places, is there such a village for roses. Apart from its flowers, I confess that the place has little worthy of notice; it cannot even show a church, because its church is within the Castle walls, and quite hidden from the village. The Castle, which, now that the long wars are over, one hopes for many years, is silent and deserted, its ruined courts empty, its crumbling walls left to decay, presented a different appearance indeed in the spring of the year 1802. For in those days it was garrisoned by two regiments of militia, and was occupied by the prodigious number of eight thousand prisoners.

"I am told that there are other ancient castles in the country even more extensive and more stately than Porchester; but I have never seen them, and am quite satisfied to believe that for grandeur, extent, and the awe of antiquity, there can be none which can surpass, and few which can pretend to equal, this monument. It is certainly ruinous in parts, yet still so strong as to serve for a great prison, but it is not overthrown, and its crumbling walls, broken roofs, and dismantled chambers surround the place with a solemnity which affects the most careless visitor.

"It is so ancient that there are some who pretend that parts of it may belong to British times, while it is certain that the whole of the outer wall was built by the Romans. In imitation of their camps, it stands four-square, and has hollow round towers in the sides and at the corners. The spot was chosen, not at the mouth of the harbour—the Britons having no means of attacking ships entering or going out—but at the very head of the harbour, where the creek runs up between the shallows, which are banks of mud at low water. Hither came the Roman galleys, laden with military stores, to land them under the protection of the Castle. When the Romans went away, and the Saxons came, who loved not fighting behind walls, they neglected the fortress, but built a church within the walls, and there laid their dead. When in their turn the Normans came, they built a castle after their own fashion, within the Roman walls. This is the stronghold, containing four square towers and a fortified entrance. And the Normans built the water-gate, and the gate-tower. The rest of the great space became the outer bailey of the Castle. They also added battlements to the wall, and dug a moat, which they filled with sea-water at high tide.

"The battlements of the Normans are now broken down or crumbling away; great patches of the rubble work have fallen here and there. Yet one can walk round the narrow ledge designed for the bowmen. The wall is crowned with waving grass and wallflowers, and up the sides grow elder-bushes, blackberry, ivy, and bramble, as luxuriantly as in any hedge beyond Portsdown. If you step out through the water-gate, which is now roofless, with little left to show its former splendour, except a single massive column, you will find, at high tide, the water lapping the lowest stones of the towers, just as it did when the Romans built them. Instead of the old galleys, which must have been light in draught to come up Porchester Creek, there are now lying half a dozen boats, the whole fleet of the little village. On the other side of the water are the wooded islets of Great and Little Horsea, and I suppose they look today much as they did a thousand years ago. On this side you look towards the east; but if you get to the south side of the Castle, and walk across a narrow meadow which lies between the wall and the sea, you have a very different view. For you look straight across the harbour to its very mouth, three miles away; you gaze upon a forest of masts and upon ships of every kind, from the stately man-o'-war to the saucy pink, and, twenty years ago, of every nation—because, in those days, we seemed at war with half the world—from the French-built frigate, the most beautiful ship that floats, to the Mediterranean xebecque, all of them prizes. Here they lie, some ready for sea, some just arrived, some battered by shot, some newly repaired and fresh from the yard; some—it seems a cruel fate for ships which have fought the battles of their country—converted into hulks for convicts and for prisoners; some store-ships—why, there is no end to the number and the kind of the ships lying in the harbour. They could tell, if they could speak, of many a battle and many a storm; some of them are as old as the days of Admiral Benbow; one poor old hulk is so old that she was once a man-o'-war in the Dutch wars of Charles II, and carried on board, it is said, the Duke of York himself."

I have put so much of my own childhood into that book that I must quote from it again presently.

Shortly after this story appeared I received a visit from a lady who told me a little anecdote and made me a little present. "In the year 1803," she said, with the solemnity and importance which belonged to what she was about to give me, "when the war broke out again and Napoleon detained all the English travellers or visitors in France, my very dear old friend X. Y. was engaged to be married. Her lover, however, who was then in Paris, was taken prisoner, although a civilian, and made to live at Verdun for eleven long years. The marriage was put off until he regained his liberty. Meantime my friend, with a fellow feeling for all prisoners, took lodgings at Portsmouth, and went by boat to Porchester Castle everyday. Here she occupied herself, being the kindest and dearest of all women, in nursing the sick prisoners until the Peace of 1814 restored her lover. Among other things which, at her death, she bequeathed me, was a collection of things made by the French prisoners, and either bought by her or given to her. Among them is a dainty little box made of straw, with a piece of looking-glass in the lid. As you have written a story about the prisoners, I have brought it, and now give it to you. I want you to give it to your eldest daughter, and I will ask her to keep it in memory of those poor prisoners and my dear friend who helped them."

A pretty story and a pretty gift. I gave it to my daughter, who keeps it among her treasures.

In childhood, however, these things were as yet distant. It was enough to climb on the gun-carriage and to look out across the harbour upon the Castle and the Hill. There were flowers on the walls: the little pimpernel; the daisy; the buttercup; the dandelion (which was not to be picked, for some superstition); and, above all, the sweet and fragrant flower that we called the wild lily—the wild convolvulus. This grew everywhere; on all the slopes and among all the bastions we gathered it by handfuls. I have always loved the perfume of this sweet flower. To this day, when I gather one of these flowers the fragrance sends me back to that old bastion, and I am once more standing, hoop in hand, looking across the harbour, my childish brain full of fancies and wonderings and vague longings, and a sense which has never left me that life is a great and wonderful gift, and that the Lord made His children for happiness. I do not say that this fine sentiment was clothed in words. But it was there—one of the long, long thoughts of childhood.

In my novel *By Celia's Arbour*, the narrator was a Pole, a son of one of the Polish exiles. I placed him under the care of a sailor's widow—a washerwoman—in order to describe the quarter; it was in Portsea, about which I rambled as a boy, looking at the odd and pretty things which the sailors brought home, and their wives put in the windows.

"Mrs. Jeram was a weekly tenant in one of a row of small four-roomed houses known as Victory Row, which led out of Nelson Street, and was a broad, blind court, bounded on one side and at the end by the Dockyard wall. It was not a dirty and confined court, but quite the reverse, being large, clean, and a very Cathedral Close for quietness. The wall, built of a warm red brick, had a broad and sloping top, on which grew wallflowers, long grasses, and stonecrop; overhanging the wall was a row of great elms, in the branches of which there was a rookery, so that all day long you could listen, if you wished, to the talk of the rooks. Now this is never querulous, angry, or argumentative. The rook does not combat an adversary's opinion; he merely states his own; if the other one does not agree with him he states it again, but without temper. If you watch them and listen, you will come to the conclusion that they are not theorists, like poor humans, but simply investigators of fact. It has a restful sound, the talk of rooks; you listen in the early morning, and they assist your sleeping half-dream without waking you; or in the evening they carry your imagination away to woods and sweet country glades. They have cut down the elms now, and driven the rooks to find another shelter. Very likely, in their desire to sweep away everything that is pretty, they have torn the wallflowers and grasses off the wall as well. And if these are gone, no doubt Victory Row has lost its only charm. If I were to visit it now, I should probably find it squalid and mean. The eating of the tree of knowledge so often makes things that once we loved look squalid.

"But to childhood nothing is unlovely in which the imagination can light upon something to feed it. It is the blessed province of all children, high and low, to find themselves at the gates of Paradise, and quite certainly Tom the Piper's son, sitting under a hedge with a raw potato for plaything, is every bit as happy as a little Prince of Wales. The possibilities of the world which opens out before us are infinite; while the glories of the world we have left behind are still clinging to the brain, and shed a supernatural colouring on everything. At six, it is enough to live; to awake in the morning to the joy of another day; to eat, sleep, play, and wonder; to revel in the vanities of childhood; to wanton in make-

WALTER BESANT

belief superiority; to admire the deeds of bigger children; to emulate them, like Icarus; and too often, like that greatly daring youth, to fall.

"Try to remember, if you can, something of the mental attitude of childhood; recall, if you may, some of the long thoughts of early days. To begin with—God was quite close to you, up among the stars; He was seated somewhere, ready to give you whatever you wanted; everybody was a friend, and everybody was occupied all day long about your personal concerns; you had not yet arrived at the boyishness of forming plans for the future. You were still engaged in imitating, exercising, wondering. Every man was a demi-god—you had not yet arrived at the consciousness that you might become yourself a man; the resources of a woman—to whom belong bread, butter, sugar, cake, and jam—were unbounded; everything that you saw was full of strange and mysterious interest. You had not yet learned to sneer, to criticise, to compare, and to down-cry.

"Mrs. Jeram's house, therefore, in my eyes, contained everything the heart of man could crave for. The green-painted door opened into a room which was at once reception-room, dining-room, and kitchen; furnished, too, though that I did not know, in anticipation of the present fashion, having plates of blue and white china stuck round the walls. The walls were built of that warm red brick which time covers with a coating of grey-like moss. You find it everywhere among the old houses of the south of England; but I suppose the clay is all used up, because I see none of it in the new houses.

"We were quite respectable people in Victory Row; of that I am quite sure, because Mrs. Jeram would have made the place much too lively, by the power and persistence of her tongue, for other than respectable people. We were seafaring folk, of course; and in every house was something strange from foreign parts. To this day I never see anything new in London shops or in museums without a backward rush of associations which lands me once more in Victory Row; for the sailors' wives had all these things long ago, before inland people ever heard of them. There were Japanese cabinets, picked up in Chinese ports long before Japan was open; there was curious carved wood and ivory work from Canton. These things were got during the Chinese war. And there was a public-house in a street hard by which was decorated, instead of with a red window-blind, like other such establishments, with a splendid picture representing some of the episodes in that struggle; all the Chinese were running away in a disgraceful stampede, while Jack Tar, running after them, caught hold of their pigtails with the left hand,

and deftly cut off their heads with the right, administering at the same time a frolicsome kick. John Chinaman's legs were generally both off the ground together, such was his fear. Then there were carved ostrich eggs; wonderful things from the Brazils in feathers; frail delicacies in coral from the Philippines, known as Venus's flower-baskets; gruesome-looking cases from the West Indies, containing centipedes, scorpions, beetles, and tarantulas; small turtle shells, dried flying-fish, which came out in moist exudations during wet weather, and smelt like haddock; shells of all kinds, big and little; clubs, tomahawks, and other queer weapons, carved in wood, from the Pacific; stuffed humming-birds, and birds of Paradise. There were live birds, too—avvadavats, Java sparrows, lovebirds, parroquets, and parrots in plenty. There was one parrot, at the corner house, which affected the ways of one suffering from incurable consumption—he was considered intensely comic by children and persons of strong stomach and small imagination. There were parrots who came, stayed a little while, and then were taken away and sold, who spoke foreign tongues with amazing volubility, who swore worse than Gresset's Vert Vert, and who whistled as beautifully as a boatswain—the same airs, too. The specimens which belonged to Art or inanimate Nature were ranged upon a table at the window. They generally stood or were grouped round a large Bible, which it was a point of ceremonial to have in the house. The live birds were hung outside in sunny weather, all except the parrot with the perpetual cold, who walked up and down the court by himself and coughed. The streets surrounding us were, like our own, principally inhabited by mariners and their families, and presented similar characteristics; so that one moved about in a great museum, open for general inspection during daylight, and free for all the world. Certain I am that if all the rare and curious things displayed in these windows had been collected and preserved, the town would have had a most characteristic and remarkable museum of its own.

"Among my early friends were one or two of the Polish exiles and refugees who lived at Portsmouth and were pensioned by our Government. The man called Wassielewski was my especial friend.

"They had a great barrack all to themselves, close to the walls, whither I used to be sometimes carried. It was a narrow building, built of black-tarred wood, with windows at both sides, so that you saw the light quite through the house.

"It stood just under the walls, almost in the shade of the great elms. Within it were upwards of a hundred Poles, living chiefly on the tenpence a day which the English Government allowed them for their support, with this barn-like structure to house them. They were desperately poor, all of them living mostly on bread and frugal cabbage-soup. Out of their poverty, out of their tenpence a day, some of these poor fellows found means by clubbing together to pay Mrs. Jeram, week by week, for my support. They went hungry that I might eat and thrive; they came everyday, some of them, to see that I was well cared for. They took me to their barrack, and made me their pet and plaything; there was nothing they were not ready to do for me, because I was the child of Roman Pulaski and Claudia his wife.

"The one who came oftenest, stayed the longest, and seemed in an especial manner to be my guardian, was a man who was grey when I first remember him. He had long hair and a full grey beard. There was a great red gash in his cheek, which turned white when he grew excited or was moved. He limped with one foot, because some musket ball had struck him in the heel; and he had singularly deep-set eyes, with heavy eyebrows. I have never seen anything like the sorrowfulness of Wassielewski's eyes. Other Poles had reason for sorrow. They were all exiles together, they were separated from their families, without a hope that the terrible Nicolas, who hated a rebel Pole with all the strength of his autocratic hatred, would ever let them return; they were all in poverty, but these men looked happy. Wassielewski alone never smiled, and carried always that low light of melancholy in his eyes, as if not only the past was sad, but the future was charged with more sorrow. On one day in the year he brought me *immortelles*, tied with a black ribbon. He told me they were in memory of my father, Roman Pulaski, now dead and in heaven, and of my mother, also dead, and now sitting among the saints and martyrs. I used to wonder at those times to see the eyes which rested on me so tenderly melt and fill with tears.

"My early childhood, spent among these kindly people, was thus very rich in the things which stimulate the imagination. Strange and rare objects in every house, in every street something from far-off lands, talk to be heard of foreign ports and bygone battles, the poor Poles in their bare and gaunt barracks, and then the place itself. I have spoken of the rookery beyond the flower-grown Dockyard wall. But beyond the rookery was the Dockyard itself, quiet and orderly, which I could see from the upper window of the house. There was the Long Row, where resided the Heads of Departments; the Short Row, in which lived functionaries of lower rank—I believe the two Rows do not know each other in society;

there was the great reservoir, supported on tall and spidery legs, beneath which stood piles of wood cut and dressed, and stacked for use; there was the Rope Walk, a quarter of a mile long, in which I knew walked incessantly up and down the workmen who turned hanks of yarn into strong cables smelling of fresh tar; there were the buildings where other workmen made blocks, bent beams, shaped all the parts of ships; there were the great places where they made and repaired machinery; there were the sheds themselves, where the mighty ships grew slowly day by day, miracles of man's constructive skill, in the dim twilight of their wooden cradles; there was a pool of sea water in which lay timber to be seasoned, and sometimes I saw boys paddling up and down in it; there was always the busy crowd of officers and sailors going up and down, some of them god-like, with cocked hats, epaulettes and swords.

"And all day long, never ceasing, the busy sound of the Yard. To strangers and visitors it was just a confused and deafening noise. When you got to know it, you distinguished half-a-dozen distinct sounds which made up that inharmonious and yet not unpleasing whole. There was the chatter of the caulkers' mallets, which never cease their tap, tap, tap, until you got used to the regular beat, and felt it no more than you feel the beating of your pulse. But it was a main part of the noise which made the life of the Yard. Next to the multitudinous mallets of the caulkers, which were like the never-ceasing hum and whisper of insects on a hot day, came the loud clanging of the hammer from the boiler-makers' shop. That might be likened, by a stretch of fancy, to the crowing of cocks in a farmyard. Then, all by itself, came a heavy thud which made the earth tremble, echoed all around, and silenced for a moment everything else. It came from the Nasmyth steam hammer; and always running through all, and yet distinct, the r-r-r-r of the machinery, like the rustling of the leaves in the wind. Of course I say nothing about salutes, because everyday a salute of some kind was thundering and rolling about the air as the ships came and went, each as tenacious of her number of guns as an Indian Rajah.

"Beyond the Dockyard—you could not see it, but you felt it, and knew that it was there—was the broad blue lake of the harbour, crowded with old ships sacred to the memory of a hundred fights, lying in stately idleness, waiting for the fiat of some ignorant and meddling First Lord ordering them to be broken up. As if it were anything short of wickedness to break up any single ship which has fought the country's battles and won her victories, until the tooth of Time, aided by barnacles, shall have rendered it impossible for her to keep afloat any longer.

WALTER BESANT

"When the last bell rang at six o'clock, and the workmen went away, all became quiet in the Dockyard. A great stillness began suddenly, and reigned there till the morning, unbroken save by the rooks which cawed in the elms, and the clock which struck the hours. And then one had to fall back on the less imaginative noises of Victory Row, where the parrot coughed, and the grass widows gathered together, talking and disputing in shrill concert, and Leonard fought Moses before going to bed, not without some din of battle."

In the same novel I have described the Common Hard, as I remember it in my childhood as follows:—

"The Common Hard, is still, after all the modern changes, a street with a distinct character of its own. The houses still look out upon the bright and busy harbour, though there is now a railway terminus and an ugly pier; though steam launches run across the water; and though there are telegraph posts, cabs, and omnibuses, all the outward signs of advanced civilisation. But thirty years ago it was a place which seemed to belong to the previous century. There were no great houses and handsome shops, but in their place a picturesque row of irregular cottages, no two of which were exactly alike, but which resembled each other in certain particulars. They were two-storeyed houses; the upper storey was very low, the ground-floor was below the level of the street. I do not know why, but the fact remains that in my town the ground-floors of all the old houses were below the level of the pavement. You had to stoop, if you were tall, to get into the doorway, and then, unless you were experienced, you generally fell headlong down a step of a foot or so. Unless the houses were shops they had only one window below and one above, because the tax on windows obliged people to economise their light. The roofs were of red tiles, high-pitched, and generally broken-backed; stone-crop and house-leek grew upon them. The Hard existed then only for the sailors. There were one or two jewellers who bought as well as sold; many public-houses, and a plentiful supply of rascally pay-agents. That side had little interest for boys. In old times the high tide had washed right up to the foot of these houses, which then stood upon the beach itself. But they built a stone wall, which kept back the water, and allowed a road to be made, protected by an iron railing. An open space gave access to what was called the 'beach,' being a narrow spit of land, along which were ranged on either side the wherries of the boatmen. A wooden bench was placed along the iron railings near the beach, on which sat everyday and all day long old sailors, in a row. It was their club, their daily rendezvous, the place where they discussed old battles, smoked pipes, and lamented bygone days. They never seemed to walk about or to care much where they sat. They sat still, and sat steadily, in hot weather and in cold. The oddest thing about this line of veterans was that they all seemed to have wooden legs. There was, or there exists in my memory, which is the same thing, a row of wooden pegs which did duty for the lost legs, sticking out straight in front of the bench when they were on it. The effect of this was very remarkable. Some, of course, had lost other outlying bits of the human frame; a hand, the place supplied by a hook, like that of Cap'en Cuttle, whose acquaintance I formed later on; a whole arm, its absence marked by the empty sleeve sewn to the front of the jersey; and there were scars in plenty. Like my friends the Poles, these heroes had gained their scars and lost their limbs in action.

"Thirty years ago we were only a quarter of a century or so from the long and mighty struggle which lasted for a whole generation, and filled this seaport town with prosperity, self-satisfaction, and happiness. Oh, for the brave old days when week after week French, American, Spanish, and Dutch prizes were towed into harbour by their victors, or sailed in, the Union Jack flying at the peak, the original crew safe under hatches, in command of a middy, and half-a-dozen British sailors told off to take her home. They talked, these old grizzle-heads, of fights and convoys, and perilous times afloat. I sat among them, or stood in front of them, and listened. Child as I was, my little heart glowed to hear how, yardarm to yardarm, they lay alongside the Frenchman; how a dozen times over the plucky little French beggars tried to board them; how she sheered off at last, and they followed, raking her fore and aft; how she suddenly broke out into flame, and before you could say 'Jack Robinson,' blew up, with all that was left of a thousand men aboard; with merry yarns of Chinese pigtails, made to be pulled by the British sailor, and niggers of Jamaica, and Dutchmen at the Cape. Also, what stories of slavers, of catching American skippers in the very act of chucking the niggers overboard, of cutting out Arab dhows, of sailing in picturesque waters where the natives swim about in the deep like porpoises; of boat expeditions up silent rivers in search of piratical Malays; of lying frozen for months in Arctic regions, long before they thought of calling men heroes for passing a single winter on the ice with every modern appliance for making things comfortable.

Here is a picture of a scene which I often witnessed—feast and merriment, mad and loud and furious, and full of things to make the moralist weep. I have stood at the open door, looking in for half an hour at a time at the sailors dancing hornpipes and the girls dancing jigs, and all singing and drinking together. Do you suppose it does a child any harm to see such things? Not a bit, so long as he knows not what such things mean; the thing is like a lovely act in a beautiful play: the music of the fiddles is heavenly, the laughter and the joy of the nymphs and sailors is like a part of Paradise. I quote from *By Celia's Arbour.*

"We came to a public-house; that one with the picture outside it of the Chinese war. There was a long, low sort of hall within it, at the end of which Wassielewski took his place, and began to fiddle again. Dancing then set in, though it was still early in the morning, with great severity. With dancing, drink; with both, songs; with all three, Wassielewski's fiddle. I suppose it was the commencement of a drunken orgie, and the whole thing was disgraceful. Remember, however, that it was more than thirty years ago, when the Navy still retained its old traditions. Foremost among them was the tradition that being ashore meant drink as long as the money lasted. It sometimes lasted a week, or even a fortnight, and was sometimes got through in a day or two. There were harpies and pirates in every house which was open to Jack. Jack, indeed, was cheated wherever he went. Afloat, he was robbed by the purser; he was ill-fed and found, the Government paying for good food and good stores, contractors and purveyors combining with the purser to defraud him. Ashore, he was horribly, shamefully cheated and robbed when he was paid off by a Navy bill, and fell into the hands of the pay agents. He was a rough-hided ruffian, who could fight, had seen plenty of fighting, was tolerably inured to every kind of climate, and ready to laugh at any kind of danger, except, perhaps, Yellow Jack. He was also tender-hearted and sentimental. Sometimes he was away for five years at a stretch, and, if his Captain chose to make it so, his life was a dog's life. Floggings were frequent; rum was the reward of good conduct; there were no Sailors' Homes, none of the many humanising influences which have made the British sailor the quiet, decorous creature, generally a teetotaller, and often inclined to a Methodist way of thinking in religion, half soldier, half sailor, that he is at present.

"It was an orgie, I suppose, at which no child should have been present. Fortunately, at half-past twelve, the landlord piped all hands for dinner."

I made friends, of course, with the veterans. Sometimes I ventured on a little offering of tobacco. One of them, a very ancient mariner, used always to declare that he had been cabin boy under Captain Cook when that great navigator was murdered. It was possible. The time when I knew this venerable old salt was about the year 1848. Cook died in 1779. If my friend was born in 1765 he might very well have been a cabin boy in 1779. And in 1848 he would have been eighty-three years of age. A good many of these old sailors lived to be past eighty. Of course, all these veterans belonged to the long wars of 1795–1815.

Another recollection. There were convict hulks in the harbour; the convicts were set to do the work of excavating, etc., for docks, and other things of the kind. Of course they were closely watched by warders armed with loaded muskets. Now there was one thing which these poor wretches ardently desired—tobacco. To give tobacco to a convict was, of course, forbidden, or to speak to him or to make any kind of communication to them. It was my practice, therefore, to get a lump of the rough, strong roll tobacco, put it in my pocket and loiter about as near to a convict as I could get without exciting suspicion. The man for his part would work in my direction; he knew perfectly well what was intended. I waited until the nearest warder had his eyes the other way, and then jerked the quid as near the convict as I could. He raised his spade and began to scrape the instrument as if something was in the way. Then he put his foot on the quid, scraped again, and stooping in the most natural way in the world, as if to get rid of a stone, he picked up the quid and continued his work— watching the warder. As soon as his eye was turned, he put the quid in his mouth, and for the remainder of that day, certainly, he was a happy man.

II

Child and Boy (continued)

Let me speak, reverently, as indeed I must, of the home life and the family circle. My father was the youngest of ten children; he was born at the beginning of the year 1800; consequently, he belonged to the eighteenth century. His father, who was in some branch of the Civil Service, died, I believe, about the year 1825. Of him I have no tradition save that he went to his club every evening—this means his tavern—returning home for supper at nine punctually; that he was somewhat austere—or was it only of uncertain temper?—and that his daughters on hearing the paternal footstep outside always retreated to bed. Out of the ten children I only know of eight. Two of them were in the Navy; one died young, the other got into some trouble and had to leave the Service—perhaps, however, he was one of the officers who were dismissed on the reduction of the Navy to a peace footing. Another entered the Civil Service and rose to a highly respectable position; he was the first of the name whose portrait was ever exhibited at the Royal Academy. Two of the daughters married, one of them a man of considerable fortune; the other an official of the Dockyard. As for my father, he tried many things. For sometime he was in very low water; then he got up again and settled in a quiet office. He was not a pushing man, nor did he know how to catch at opportunities. Mostly, he waited. Meantime he was a studious man, whose chief delight was in reading; he was especially well acquainted with the English drama, from Shakespeare to Sheridan; and he had a good collection of plays, which he parted with when he thought that they might do harm to his boys. I had, however, by that time read them all, and I am sure that they never did any harm to me. He was a shy man, and very retiring; he never went into any kind of society; he belonged to no Masonic Lodge or other fraternity: he would not take any part in municipal affairs; he was fond of gardening, and had a very good garden, in which he spent the greater part of every morning; and he asked for nothing more than an occasional visit in the afternoon from a friend and an evening quiet and free from interruption.

He was never in the least degree moved by the Calvinistic fanaticism of the time. So called "religious" people, those who had been under "conviction," the "Lord's People" (as they arrogantly called themselves), were very much exercised about the Elect, their limited number, and the extreme uncertainty that any of their friends belonged to that select body. As for themselves, of course, they had no doubt. What was the meaning of Conviction unless it was also Election? The Devils, they would say, believe and tremble. Assuredly they were not Devils. Therefore—but the conclusion was illogical. Now my father took the somewhat original line of sticking to the rules and regulations. "The Lord," he said, "has laid down Rules plain and simple. There they are, written up on the wall of the Church and read out every Sunday for everybody to hear. Very good; I keep these Rules, and I go to Church every Sunday out of respect to the Almighty who drew up those Rules. No more can be expected of any man. As for what they talk, my boy, they can't talk away the plain Rules—because there they are; and I don't find that the man who keeps those Rules is going to be damned, but quite the contrary." I have often wondered at this singular attitude, which was so entirely contrary to the habit of the time. But then my father did not altogether belong to the time. Although regular in attendance at church, he never ventured to present himself at Holy Communion. In this respect he did follow his own generation, in which the participation in the Sacrament was a profession of peculiar sanctity. Since we were warned how we might, by unworthily partaking, cause our own damnation, it was generally felt that it was wiser not to run the risk.

When I consider the extent of the Calvinistic teaching; its dreadful narrowness; the truly heartless and pitiless way in which those solemn faces above the wobbling Geneva bands spoke of the small number of the Elect and the certainty of endless torment for the multitude—the whole illustrating the ineffable Love of God—I am amazed that people were as cheerful as they were. I suppose that people were accustomed to this kind of talk; there was no question of rebellion; nobody dared to doubt or disbelieve; only, you see, the doctrine if realised would have made life intolerable; the human affections only the source and spring of agony; religion a selfish, individual, doubtful hope; the closing years of old age a horrible anticipation of what was to follow. Therefore the thing was put away in silence; it was brought out in two sermons every week; it was regarded as a theological exercise in which the congregation could admire the intellectual subtleties by which every gracious word of Christ was, by some distortion of half a verse from Paul, turned into the exact opposite of what it meant. For my own part, I now understand what an excellent discipline the Sunday services were. No getting out of it on any terms; two services and at each a sermon an hour long and sometimes more—doctrinal, Evangelical and Calvinistic. One had to sit quite still and awake; not to wriggle; not to whisper; not to titter. As for the sermon itself, I enjoyed it very much. Of course I understood very early that the sermon had no bearing on my own conduct nor on any prospects I might have entertained concerning the life to come. Indeed, after I had read the Book of Revelation, which I did early, I disconnected Heaven altogether from the man with the white bands, and made up my mind that he was talking about something which was quite unconnected with the Apostle of Patmos—as indeed was the case. In church, therefore, I found many consolations for the length of the service. During the Litany and the Prayers I could bury my face in my hands and go off in dreams and imaginations—they were dreams of delight. During the sermon I could drop my eyes and carry on these dreams. To this day I can never listen to a sermon. The preachers begin—I try to give them a chance. Then the old habit returns. Involuntarily my eyes drop, I fly away, I am again John-o'-dreams. Perhaps that is the reason why I have not been to church, except once or twice, for nearly thirty years. I except the Cathedral service, which does not mean a sermon. I go into St. Paul's or Westminster if I am passing by, and sit in a corner till the anthem is over. Then I get up and walk out, my soul refreshed with the prayer and praise of the choir and organ.

It was another great stroke of good luck—see what good things were provided for me by Fortune!—that we had a small library. Very few middleclass people in my childhood had any books to speak of, except a few shelves filled with dreary divinity or old Greek and Latin Classics. We had an excellent collection of books. There were, I remember, *Don Quixote*, *Robinson Crusoe*, Bunyan's works, Marryat's works, and those of Dickens which were then written; all Miss Edgeworth's books, Hume and Smollett's *History*, Conder's *Traveller*, the *Spectator* and the *Guardian*; Sterne's works, and some of Swift's; Pope's *Homer* and some of his other poems; Goldsmith's works complete; the Waverley Novels; Byron, Wordsworth, and a number of minor poets; whole shelves of plays; some volumes of an Encyclopædia; two volumes, very useful to me, called *Elegant Extracts*; histories of France, Rome, and Greece; Washington Irving's works, and a good many others. Besides which, I saved up my pocket-money and belonged to the "Athenæum," which had a small lending library. For a boy who loved books beyond and above everything, here was a collection that lasted till I was twelve, at least. I was encouraged to read not only by my father's example, but by my mother's exhortations and approval. She saw in learning a hope for the future; she had ambitions for her boys, though she kept these ambitions to herself.

Let me speak once for all about my mother. She was a New Forest girl, born and brought up in a village called Dibden, near Hythe and Beaulieu (Bewlay). The church stands actually in the Forest; a peaceful, quiet church, to which I once paid a pilgrimage. My mother was the youngest of a large family. During her childhood she ran about on the outskirts of the Forest, catching and riding the bare-backed ponies, and drinking in the folklore and old-wife wisdom of that sequestered district. At eighteen years of age, I think in 1825, she married and came to Portsmouth to live. Her father was not a New Forest man; he came from Lincolnshire, his name being Eddis. Her mother belonged to an old New Forest race of farmers or yeomen named Nowell. Her father was by trade or profession a builder, contractor, and architect. Some portions of Hurst Castle were built by him. I imagine that his business lay chiefly in Southampton, and that his family lived for convenience of country air across the water. He died comparatively young, and his large family seems to have dwindled down to a very few descendants, one branch of whom alone is known to me at the present moment.

My mother was the cleverest woman I have ever known: the quickest witted; the surest and safest in her judgments; the most prophetic for those she loved; the most far-seeing. Her education had been what you might expect in a village between the years 1807, when she was born, and 1825, when she married. But it sufficed—because it was not book-learning that she wanted for the care and upbringing of the children, for whom she rose early and worked late. I have said that ours was a household in which economy had to be practised, but without privation. The comfort of the house, the well-being of the children, were alike due to my mother's genius for administration. Imagine, if you can, her pride and joy when her eldest child, her eldest son, took prizes and scholarships at Cambridge; was first, year after year, in his college examinations, and finished by becoming senior wrangler and first Smith's Prizeman! It was my happiness, twenty years afterwards, to make her proud of her third son, who was gaining some success in other fields. When I think of such imaginative gifts as I have possessed, I go back in memory to the old times when we sat at my mother's feet in blindman's holiday, when the sun had gone down, but the lights were not brought in, and she would tell us stories of the New Forest; when I, for one, would listen, gazing into the red coals and seeing, as in a procession, the figures of the story pass before me and act their parts between the bars. She gave me such imaginative powers as have enabled me to play my part as a novelist; it is my inheritance from her. To others of her children she gave other gifts; to one the mathematical mind; to another a marvellous memory and a grasp of figures quite remarkable; to a third she gave the rapid mind which seizes facts and jumps at conclusions while others are groping after the main issues; to another she gave the eye and the hand of the artist—though this gift was unhappily wasted.

When I grew older I began to desire to see things of which the books that I had read were full. Now Portsea Island is excellently placed to give a boy a right understanding of the sea and of ships, and of the folk who go upon the sea in ships; but it is a perfectly flat island, nowhere more than a few feet above the high tide level; there are no streams upon it; there are no woods; there are no hills; there are no villages; there are no village churches; there is no pleasant country. Only in one place, on the east side where they once began to make a canal leading from nothing to nowhere, there is a wild tract of land looking out across Langston Harbour, a lagoon on whose broad bosom there are no ships, and the only boats are the duck hunters' broad flat craft with outriggers. Beyond the island, however, and on the mainland, there was another kind of country, a Delectable Land.

When I was about twelve or so it was a joy to me to walk four miles to the little village of Cosham, on the mainland, and so over Portsdown Hill into the lovely country beyond; the lane led past a picturesque old church, concealed among the trees and far from any village. I have found many Hampshire churches hidden away in woods far from any hamlet. The church of Rowner, near Gosport, that of Widley, behind Portsdown, that of Dibden, near Hythe, where my mother's people are buried, occur to me. I suppose that the parishes were large, and that the church, having to serve several hamlets, was placed in a spot most convenient for all. It was at Widley Church that I first felt the charm of things ancient. To sit in a lonely churchyard among trees and mouldering mounds, and to gaze upon a venerable house which has soothed and consoled generations—say from the time when King Alfred brought back the scattered priests to Wessex—to be all alone, with the imagination of a child and the knowledge of a bookish boy; to feed the imagination with the long thoughts of childhood, was a kind of ecstasy. It seemed as if I was nearer the gates of heaven than I have ever since attained—

> —*"but now 'tis little joy*
> *To find that heaven is farther off*
> *Than when I was a boy."*

Beyond the church, the lane led to a stream—the first stream I had ever seen, bright, swift, babbling and bubbling over the stones. Over it grew the trees—I forget what trees—indeed, I knew not then what they were; a fallen branch lay across the stream; dragon flies gleamed in bright flashes over the water; the forest was loud with the song of birds; the heavy bumble-bee droned about the flowers; and I am sure that there were more butterflies, especially the little blue ones—perhaps the prettiest of all—than I have seen elsewhere. I should be afraid to go to Widley Church again. I should perhaps find it restored or rebuilt; and perhaps the lane has houses in it. Let it remain a memory.

I was therefore a town lad—or a seaport lad; the things of Nature, the birds, the flowers, the trees, the woods, the stream, the creatures, were not, so to speak, a part of me. To begin with, I was always shortsighted. I therefore saw little of the endless variety in form, colour, and curve. The shapes of the leaves; the variations of the flowers; the flight and the differences of the birds; the small things of Nature; these I have never seen, to my infinite loss. I went among the woods as a stranger; I had no plant lore, wild flower lore, wood lore; I have never acquired any. In all the years since then I have read but little in the book of Nature. In the printed book, to be sure, I have read a great deal about Nature. It is something, but not everything. And as regards Nature I do not know whether it is better to read of what you know or of what you know nothing. Richard Jefferies walks along a hedge and talks to me. It is like the uplifting of a veil; I am conscious that my senses are imperfect; I am not only short-sighted but I am slow-sighted; it takes time for me to make out things clearly. Again, in the sense of smell I have not, I am convinced, anything like the acuteness of those who have lived much in the country. I have a companion (who has tried to teach me all she knows), who finds, I am aware, a thousand breaths of fragrance where I find only one. She hears in the warbling of the woods a hundred notes, and distinguishes them all—to me they are mostly alike; she knows all the trees, with the infinite varieties of leaf, of colour, of bough and branch, with the loveliness and the charm that belong to each—I take them all together; she knows all the wild flowers and loves them everyone for its own sake and for its own special charm—I love them all together. This comes of a childhood spent in streets and on the seashore; and of a boyhood wherein the leisure hours were chiefly passed coiled up in a corner, nose in book.

In recalling those days it is difficult to separate them from the imaginary characters of my novel—*By Celia's Arbour*. When I think of the Dockyard I see the two boys, Ladislas and Leonard, peering into the twilight of the long rope-walk; being launched on board a three-decker; rowing about in the mast pond; watching the semaphore and trying to read its signals; looking into the building-sheds and standing aside to let the Port Admiral pass. When I think of Southsea Common, I see an open heath behind a bank of shingle and sand, with a marsh and a tiny rivulet on one side and a broader marsh on the other; and, standing by itself, the grey old castle on the shore. It is not myself who is running across that heath, but those two boys, who share between them my identity; one is tall and handsome, with a brave and gallant air; the other is short and hump-backed. These two boys take my place on the beach and plunge side by side through the breakers; they row out to Spithead on summer evenings after sunset, when the grey twilight falls upon the sea, and no knell of the bell buoy saddens the soul; they pull that dead man out of the water whom once I found rolled over and over on the shingle; they row about among the hulks and worn out ships up the harbour; they stand on the "logs" and watch the man-o'-war's boat come alongside under charge of the little middy, who marches along the wooden pier with so much pride, the object of envy and of longing.

The boys are imaginary; the real hero of that story "the Captain" is not. To thy memory, dear old Captain, let me write one more line. He was the friend of all boys; he was the benefactor of many boys; he pulled them out of the gutter, and had them taught and sent them into the Navy; and this silently, so that his left hand knew not what was done by his right hand. There were women whom he pulled out of the lowest gutters and befriended—but I know not how; to me and mine he was a kind of "pal," to use the word which then we knew not; he understood children and he understood boys. We talked freely together, as a young boy with an old boy. In winter the Captain was dressed all in blue, with the navy button; in summer he wore white ducks, a white waistcoat, and a big coat with the navy button—the crown and anchor. I think that he wore this half-pay uniform on Sundays only. On other days he was in mufti. He was a bachelor, and lived in a house overlooking the mill-dam. At church his pew was next to ours; and as we were too many for our square box, we overflowed into his long box. The hymn books, I remember, were locked up in a receptacle at the end of the pew. When the hymns were given out he produced a bunch of keys. "Get out the tools, my boy," he would say in a loud whisper; "they are now going to squall." I never understood his objection to the hymns, but I think he disliked the assistance of a paid choir. To be sure, it was a very bad choir, and the squalling was slow and prolonged. The Captain's behaviour in church was in other respects exemplary. He sat bolt upright, preserving the appearance of attention in the same attitude for the Litany as for the sermon. Church, for him, as to most old sailors, was part of the day's duty; the performance of duty qualified the soul for promotion; a simple religion, but one which works admirably in every branch of both Services, and should, I think, be transplanted into the life of the civilian.

The church was large, and contained galleries; the living was small, but the incumbent during the forties was a fine scholar, at one time Fellow of his college at Oxford, who had taken the church coupled with a school which was then attached to it. The school was, I think, founded with the church about the year 1730. Unfortunately it was not endowed. My father was educated at this school, and so were his brothers. Among his fellow-scholars and private friends was the late Sir Frederick Madden, the great antiquary. The school somehow or other—I know not why—went to pieces, somewhere in the forties.

The Rev. H. A——, the "perpetual curate"—an excellent and historical title,—was a short, sturdy man of corpulent habit and a very red face. He had an aggressive way of walking; he marched about fearlessly in all the courts and slums, of which there were many. He was of the school then called "High"—and I believe that he was as far above his brethren, who were all Evangelical, in ecclesiastical history as he was in Latin and Greek. Afterwards I learned more about him. He had been captain of Westminster school; at Oxford he had distinguished himself in the noble art of self-defence, and was champion light bruiser. That accounted for his aggressive walk. He also distinguished himself by his scholarship. His sermons were written in excellent English. I have a volume of them still. He was further remarkable for a fine and discriminating taste in port; such small additions as he made to his slender stipend by private tuition were expended, I have reason to believe, in that most excellent of wines.

I heard, long years after, a piece of scandal concerning this scholar, which I repeat because it explains the man. In a book of small edification called the *Memoirs of Harriette Wilson,* there occurs what may be called an episode in the life of a noble lord. Harriette was one of a large family of daughters, all beautiful, who were one after the other placed by the thoughtfulness of their parents under the protection of certain noblemen and gentlemen. The youngest sister, for Instance, was sold to Lord B——, an aged person who retained the habits of his youth. Harriette relates how the girl went off crying and refused to be comforted, even when her sisters reminded her of the brilliant position she was about to occupy. However, she succeeded in making her protector marry her, and was left a very young widow. She resided at Melton Mowbray, and Mr. H. A——, then a young don at Oxford, was accustomed to pay visits of condolence and consolation to her. I daresay it was not true, but the story somehow raised the subject of it in my estimation. A man incapable of love is only half a man; a man who has loved, if not wisely, is still a man.

My first school was kept by three sisters, daughters of a retired naval surgeon. It was a cheerful school, and we all laughed a good deal. Two of the sisters were "serious," in the Evangelical language of the day; they had received "conviction"; in the words of the preacher, they were of the "Lord's people." The other, who was the eldest, was never "serious"; she was a clever, thoughtful, kindly woman. She was a lifelong friend of my sisters, and married D. A——, who, as I have said, used to accompany us every year to Porchester.

My first independent reading was *Robinson Crusoe,* to which was added *Pilgrim's Progress*, the Book of Revelation, and certain tracts. How I came to read the Book of Revelation I do not know; it terrified me horribly, while it attracted me. As regards the tracts, I suppose they were brought to the house by some of our "serious" friends. One of them spoke of a soul winging its flight to heaven, and I remember watching the tombs, especially those which were old and broken, in the hope of seeing with my own eyes a soul wing its flight to heaven. But I never did.

At the age of nine I was sent as a private pupil to the Rev. H. A——, already mentioned. He made me begin Greek and Latin at the same time. I had to learn by heart great quantities of Virgil and Homer before I could construe them. I also learned grammar in vast quantities. Most of the work was learning by heart and repetition. When I began to translate, which was very soon, my tutor took me along at a rapid rate; I acquired a fair vocabulary, and learned to translate both Latin and Greek with commendable facility. Also I began to do Latin verses as soon as I could string a few words together.

One thing I really could not approve in my experience of H. A——. It was his determination to drive the Church Catechism into my head. Every Monday morning I had to repeat the whole of it. Now for some perverse reason, although I could rattle off miles of Virgil and Homer, I could never get through the Catechism without breaking down. Generally it was in the answer to the question—"What desirest thou in the Lord's Prayer?" There I met my fate; there I broke down; the cane was at hand—Whack! whack!

I stayed with this tutor for two years or more. I declare that when I left him, at twelve years of age, I knew more Latin and Greek, I could write better verses, I could translate more readily than when I was eighteen. Alas! had I continued with him for three or four years longer, he would have made me, I am certain, a fine scholar. But I left him.

There had been, formerly, a grammar school at Portsmouth. It was endowed, I think, with an income of £200 a year; but in my time it was in decay; very few boys went to it, and I am not certain whether it was still kept up. In Portsea there had been a grammar school—St. George's Grammar School—this was now closed. A new school had been created at Southsea, called St. Paul's Grammar School. It was a "proprietary" school, under a committee. It was founded about the year 1830, I believe, and had some reputation for turning out good scholars. My brother, the best man that ever came out of the school, was the captain in 1846, going to Cambridge in October of that year. In 1848, I was taken from my private tutor and placed at St. Paul's. I was then twelve years of age, and on account of my good Latin and Greek was put at once into the Fifth, among the boys of sixteen or seventeen. They used to bully me a little because I was very small and young, and I was generally at the top. The "head" had taken a fair place in mathematical honours, but, oh! the difference in the classics! There was no more learning by heart; there was no more translating rapidly and with enthusiasm; the Latin verses were scamped. The school was ill-taught; the masters quarrelled; the boys were caned all day long. I think it must have been a good thing for everybody when the committee, I know not why, agreed to shut up the school. They sold the building for a Wesleyan chapel, which it has continued to be until the present day. By this time I knew considerably less of Greek and Latin than when I left my tutor. On the other hand there were gains. There were games, and fights; the boys fought continually. And I made a beginning with mathematics; my former tutor, poor man! could hardly add up, and knew nothing of algebra or Euclid.

The school was closed, and masters and boys dispersed, multivious. I do not think that in after life I ever came across any of those who had been boys with me at that school. The French master, however, remained a friend of ours until his death, a great many years after, at a very advanced age. I have introduced him in a story called *All in a Garden Fair*, as a teacher of French in a girls' school:—

"He was a little man, though his daughter looked as if she would be tall; yet not a very little man. His narrow sloping shoulders—a feature one may remark more often in Paris than in London—his small head, and the neatness of his figure made him look smaller than he was. Small Englishmen—this man was a Frenchman— are generally sturdy and broad-shouldered, and nearly always grow fat when they reach the forties. But this was a thin man. In appearance he was extremely neat; he wore a frock-coat buttoned tightly; behind it was a white waistcoat; he had a flower in his button-hole; he wore a pink and white necktie, very striking; his shirt-front and cuffs were perfect; his boots were highly polished; he was five-and-forty, but looked thirty; his hair was quite black and curly, without a touch of white in it; he wore a small black beard; his eyes were also black, and as bright as steel. It is perhaps misleading to compare them with steel, because it is always the villain whose eye glitters like steel. Now M. Hector Philipon was not a villain at all—by no means. The light in his eyes came from the kindness of his heart, not from any villainous aims or wicked passions, and in fact, though his beard and his hair were so very black—black of the deepest dye, such as would have graced even a wicked uncle—he frightened nobody, not even strangers. And of course everybody in those parts knew very well that he was a most harmless and amiable person. He had a voice deep and full, like the voice of a church organ; honey-sweet, too, as well as deep. And at sight of his little girl those bright eyes became as soft as the eyes of a maiden in love. When he spoke, although his English was fluent and correct, you perceived a foreign accent. But he had been so long in the country, and so far away from his own countrymen, that the accent was slight."

I was then sent, for a stop-gap, to a private school, recently opened by a clergyman who had been a dissenting minister, sometime a student, at Homerton. He was a kindly man, most anxious to do well by his boys, but unfortunately no scholar and no teacher. His school I believe lasted only for two or three years, when he gave it up and became chaplain to a gaol. I have nothing to record of the eighteen months spent with him, except that I forgot more of my Latin and Greek, and having very little to do for school work, I read pretty nearly everything that there was in the house to read.

A boy who is ignorant of things may read the worst books in the world without harm. For my own part, I read, Tristram Shandy through with the keenest delight. I adored the Captain and Corporal Trim, I found Dr. Slop delightful; as to the *double entendre* with which this work is crammed from beginning to end, I understood nothing, not a single word. When, in after years, I took up the book again, I was amazed at the discovery of what was really meant in passages which had amused me even in my ignorance.

This childish ignorance may sometimes lead one into strange confusions. I was one afternoon reading Walter Scott's *Peveril of the Peak* when two ladies called. After a few minutes of "manners"—*i.e.*, I put down the book and sat bolt upright with folded hands—as no one noticed me I relapsed into the book, became absorbed, and forgot that anyone was present. Presently I came upon a passage at which I burst out laughing.

"What is your book, dear boy?" asked one of the visitors. "Will you read us the amusing passage?"

The words were as follows. Alice was in the presence of the king. "Your Majesty," she said, "if indeed I kneel before King Charles, is the father of your subjects." "Of a good many of them," said the Duke of Buckingham, apart.

The passage was an unfortunate one. I laughed because the immensity of the family tickled me. And in reading it again, I burst out into a fresh and inextinguishable laugh. Suddenly I became aware that no one else laughed, and that all faces were stony and all eyes directed into unconscious space. I stopped laughing with many blushes. But why no one laughed I could not tell. When they were gone I ran to my own room and read the passage again and again. I laughed till I cried. But I felt guilty, and I could not tell why no one else laughed—"Of a good many of them!" What a family! I am certain, however, that I was regarded ever after by those ladies, who did know what his Grace of Buckingham meant, as a boy of strange and precocious vice.

After a time it was recognised that if I were to be perfectly equipped for the university and for holy orders I must no longer stay at this worthy person's private academy. For some reason or other I had always said that when I grew up I should be a clergyman. I should have preferred being a midshipman, but that was not possible when one was grown up. A clergyman—not that I had the least feeling of the responsibilities and the sacred character of the profession; but it was clearly a beautiful thing to put on a white robe and make everybody sit quiet and orderly, and mute as mice while he read. My mother, like many women, was pleased to think that one of her children should take holy orders, and my decision was accepted as the sign of a true vocation. It was accepted, in fact, by myself as well as by my folk until, at the age of twenty-four, I made the discovery which forbade the fulfilment of my early promise. Had the prophet Samuel seceded from the temple, his mother Hannah would not have grieved more than my mother to think that her ambitions for me in this direction were closed.

III

School-Boy

In the year 1851 I was sent to a London suburban school, Stockwell Grammar School, chosen, I believe, because one of my brother's college friends had been there and recommended it. The school was one of a small group founded in the thirties and scattered about the suburbs, much nearer the City than would now be considered a good situation. They were "in connection" with King's College, London, and exclusively Anglican. The connection amounted to a yearly examination conducted by King's College, a yearly prize, and certain small privileges if one went from the school to the College. At our school it was considered the proper thing to go on to King's College, and there to take one of the scholarships. We did this nearly every year, for a good many years; and for a small school we really did wonderfully well at Cambridge afterwards, always in the mathematical tripos. Among the old boys of this small suburban school I may mention the late Sir George Grove, Director of the Royal College of Music; Sir Henry Harben, the statistician; the Rev. Charles Voysey, of the Theistic Church; W.H.H. Hudson, Professor of Mathematics at King's College, London; Horace William Smith, Fellow of Trinity College, Cambridge; Arthur N. Wollaston, C.I.E., the Oriental Scholar; Sir Henry Irving, the actor; and Charles Irving, C.M.G., late Auditor-General of the Straits Settlements and Resident Councillor of Malacca and Penang. For the rest, we had a good sprinkling of lawyers and clergymen, together with a solid phalanx of substantial City men. This is not a bad average in the thirty years' life of an insignificant school.

There were about one hundred and twenty boys when I went there as a boarder with the headmaster. He was a graduate of some distinction in classical honours at Trinity College, Dublin; he was a solid scholar, but certainly not a fine scholar. His methods were of the old fashioned kind—the cast-iron kind—the boys were put through daily grammar and exercises, construing and parsing. The method as an educational discipline was no doubt admirable, but it gave no command of the language. Unfortunately the same method was applied to Greek and to French. It did not occur to schoolmasters of that time that our own language afforded ample scope for this kind of discipline, and that in Greek and French we might at least have been taught the language, leaving the syntax to take care of itself. I believe that the same ridiculous pretence at teaching French is still kept up; in our time we read Corneille and Racine. Imagine the usefulness of Racine in teaching modern French! The greatest linguist I have ever known began always with finding out the group of words in which a language might be said to begin: the common words—their likenesses and differences. He then began to translate; as for the grammar, he picked it up as he went along. Now in French there are three things necessary: (1) to read it easily, (2) to write it, and (3) to speak it. It is impossible to speak a language perfectly by any amount of study in an English school; nor can one learn to write it without a vocabulary. I learned French by reading it at home. Greek I could have learned in the same manner, but not writing Greek verses. However, we had the customary stumbling through so many lines of construing everyday; we had no teaching in literature or history, only grammar, parsing, and writing of exercises. Verses we did, of course, but the "head" was not strong in either Greek or Latin verses.

He was a good man and kindly, but his best qualities were concealed by an extraordinary nervousness; he had the greatest difficulty in speaking in public; if he preached, he read a ponderous discourse in an even monotone; he went into no kind of society; he had no friends. If a school can be advanced by the social qualities of its chief, then were we indeed in a bad way; no one was ever invited to the house; he spent all his evenings in his study, and his own amusement was in translating for Bohn's Library, to which he contributed three or four volumes.

On one occasion he dropped into verse. He wrote a poem in blank verse. The subject was Geology. Dr. Johnson once said that the "Mediterranean Sea" was an excellent subject for a poem; it remains for someone to act on the suggestion. Geology may also be described as an excellent subject for a poem. I wonder if there is, anywhere, a copy to be procured of this effusion. Why my master wrote it, why he published it, what golden visions fired his brain with thoughts of fame, I know not. I am certain that he must himself have paid for the production. Publication, in the proper sense, it never had, because no bookseller ever showed it or offered it. If aspiring poets only realised this point, there would be a decrease in the printing of new poems. In after years I remember a man who had published a volume of verse at his own expense revealing the terrible truth to me of his own experience. Three copies of his book had been sold, two to his own brothers! One copy represented the whole of the Anglo-Saxon demand for that volume of verse. I once asked the publisher about it. He remembered nothing at all, neither the poem nor the poet. My master's poem on Geology was written and printed, but genuine publication it lacked.

Stockwell, where our school was situated, was at that time a very good quarter, with many wealthy merchants and professional men and civil servants living in it. The place lay between the Clapham Road and the Brixton Road; it consisted of a dozen roads, all lined with stucco-fronted villas, large or small, in their gardens; the roads were planted with trees; the gardens with flowering shrubs; a leafy, peaceful, prosperous place. The boys looked to the City for their careers; but as merchants, stockbrokers, underwriters and principals, not as clerks. A few entered the professions, but not many. Clapham Common furnished one cricket ground; football was not yet played; for the smaller boys there was a playground on either side of the school.

In course of time the neighbourhood began to decay; the wealthy merchants and the professional men and city solicitors moved farther out; smaller houses were put up; a commercial education was desired rather than a classical; the school decayed. In 1870 or 1871 my old friend the head-master resigned. Then happened a terrible tragedy. He was about sixty-seven years of age; he had saved little or nothing; he fell into anxieties about the future; and one day—no one knows why— no one can offer any theory—he murdered his wife. He was tried and found guilty. There was no defence; there was no cause discovered, not the least shadow of a cause; jealousy was out of the question from one of his age towards a wife as old; no one has ever been able to suggest any probable or possible cause of the crime. Meantime people were greatly moved about it. The man was old; he was a clergyman; his life had been blameless; he was always, as a schoolmaster, kindly and good-tempered; he never fell into rages with the boys. The doctors, for their part, would not certify that he was insane. In the end they kept him in prison—but not at Broadmoor; and some years later he died in his convict's cell.

The mathematical master was a very different man. He was cheerful and jovial; he was also a very good teacher of his subject. He obtained a close fellowship at Cambridge, and went back there, lived in his college for the rest of his life, and became well known for his breezy conversation and his cultivation of the art of dining.

When I recall the boys who were there with me, two or three only stand out in my memory as remarkable. There were two brothers, Cubans, sent to England in order to learn English. They taught me the implacable hatred which the Cuban feels for the Spaniard; they longed to get back in order to take part in the next rebellion, and to help in driving the Spaniards into the sea. I wonder if they lived to see the deliverance of their island and its transference to another and a greater Power.

There was another boy who, I now understand, must have been a Eurasian. His story was very strange. On his arrival from India he was received into the house of a certain very well-known member of Parliament, financier and politician, who for some years, I believe until his death, paid the boy's school bills. He had no other friend in England and none, so far as he knew, in India. He never went away for the holidays, and as he was not an engaging youth, no one ever invited him. It was a lonely, miserable boyhood. Now it happened that about the year 1855 his patron died. It was then intimated that there was no more money; that the boy could not, therefore, as he had been always led to expect, be brought up to a profession, but must learn a trade. So after having gone through five or six years of the classical mill, with associates all intended for the liberal professions or for the better side of the City, the boy was taken away and apprenticed to a watchmaker. When his time was expired he called upon his old master, received from him whatever facts he knew connected with his history, and said that he was going back to India, in order to find his father and his own people. The facts were few indeed, only that the financier had formerly certain near relations somewhere or other in India. So he disappeared. I wonder if he ever did find his father; or if he still wanders about that broad country seeking and finding not.

Another boy I remember. He started life after leaving school with every chance, as it appeared, of a prosperous career; he succeeded to the management of a great business; was thought certain to become a very rich man; he was a member of a City company; he would speak of ambitions connected with the Mansion House itself. After he left I saw no more of him; but in course of time I heard rumours of incompetence; then of dismissal; he had been turned out of his managing directorship. His chance was gone. I lost sight of him altogether and forgot his existence, until many years later, when my name was tolerably well known as a novelist. I then received a letter in which this old schoolfellow, bursting into a gush of affection and reminiscence, told me his story as he wished it put, artlessly betraying a variegated career of failure, and ending with a request that I would at once send him £200, and would also write him a "long and chatty letter," as from an old and still affectionate friend. He wanted, you see, a testimonial of respectability. What he would have done with the letter, had I fallen into the trap, would have been to show it about and to use it, probably, for purposes of deception.

However, most of the boys, I believe, turned out well; those who are still living are substantial, but they are very few. I met one the other day, to whom the City has been a Tom Tiddler's Ground. "Have you heard," he said, "that Lawrence is dead?" Lawrence, one of the last of the schoolfellows, boy or man, was always called by his Christian name. So Lawrence was dead, and there was another link snapped.

There were many curious and pleasant places within reach of Stockwell. Clapham Common, on the south, the first of the Surrey heaths. It was surrounded by stately mansions, sacred to the memory of Wilberforce, Thornton, and Macaulay, standing amidst broad lawns with splendid cedars. The common itself was left absolutely untouched; winter water-ways made little ravines; there were ponds, there were no roads, there was gorse and fern. It was our playground. Beyond lay Wandsworth Common, another wild heath with a lake called the Black Sea wherein, it was rumoured, gigantic pike attacked and bit great holes in the boy who ventured to swim across.

On the west one could easily reach the Battersea Fields. As I recollect this place, it was most dreary and miserable; a broad flat, lower than the river, and protected by an embankment. On the bank stood the once famous Red House tavern, now long forgotten, and beside it the pigeon-shooting ground. This sport went on continually. If a pigeon escaped he was potted by men who carried guns and lay waiting for him outside the grounds. Battersea Church was on the wall of the Fields, the transformation of a great part of which into Battersea Park took place between 1851 and 1858.

In summer our favourite rambles were farther afield, in the direction of Champion Hill, Herne Hill, Dulwich, and even Penge. No one visiting these places at the present day can understand their loveliness before they were built over. Dulwich, with its ancient college and its inn, its greenery and its orchards, was surely the sweetest village in the world. I always looked about in case I might come upon Mr. Pickwick, who was then a resident, but I was never privileged to see him. The hanging woods of Penge in autumn were lovely beyond the power of words. Its Common on the Hill had been enclosed long before—in 1824—Howe laments the fact in that year; but in the fifties Penge, Norwood and Sydenham formed a group of suburbs still rural, still covered with woods and gardens, and as beautiful as any country village. As yet there were neither omnibuses nor railway. The people who went into the City drove in their own carriages or rode their own horses. Any morning along the Clapham Road there were still many who rode into town.

We were not great at games at the school. There was a cricket club, but my short sight disqualified me from any game of ball; in the winter there was hockey on Clapham Common. I think that football had not yet come in; in fact athletics, in such schools as this was, hardly existed. On the other hand we took long walks; we walked to Richmond, and rode ponies in the Park; we walked to Putney, and took boats on the River; we jumped the Effra, in the Dulwich Fields; we had a gymnastic bar and did things of strength; sometimes we wrestled; sometimes we fought. On the whole it was a healthy kind of life, with plenty of outdoor exercise.

For my own part, I had a form of recreation all my own, of which I said nothing, because the other boys would not understand it. I had friends at Camberwell and Brixton, who asked me two or three times a term to dinner on a half-holiday. On such occasions I used to get away at two and walk all the way into the City of London, which was to me then, as it has been ever since, a place of mystery, full of things to be discovered. Nothing could be more delightful than to wander about, not knowing where, so long as one was in the City. Sometimes I would light upon St. Paul's, and hear the service; sometimes, but rarely, I would find a City church open; sometimes I would climb the Monument in order to look down upon the labyrinth of streets. Sometimes I found myself in streets that I knew: Paternoster Row—that was the place of books, and I regarded the narrow lane with awe and longing; or in Little Britain—I knew that street from Washington Irving; or in Newgate Street, which was then one long double row of butchers' shops; or by the old bastion of London Wall; or in Cloth Fair, then a lovely monument of picturesque gables, overhanging windows and dirt of Tudor antiquity. Once I found myself in Goswell Street, and looked about for Mrs. Bardell, just as beside the Monument I looked about for the residence of Mrs. Todgers, or the square in which Tim Linkinwater lived. If I could only remember the City as it was! But nothing is more difficult to recall than the aspect of a street or a house before destruction and rebuilding.

It was in the summer of 1854 that I became captain of the school and left it with a barrowful of prizes. It was a small triumph, I daresay, to be captain of a little suburban school with a hundred boys, but it pleased everybody, including myself. As for what I knew—well, I believe I had less real knowledge of Latin and Greek than at twelve, but I suppose I knew more grammar. My mathematical knowledge was much better; we had gone through most of the subjects then known as the "three day" subjects, because they covered the ground of the first three days of the Cambridge mathematical tripos; and what was more, I knew them very fairly, through the accident of being taught mathematics more intelligently and with more heart than classics. I was taken out of my proper line, which was certainly the latter, and made to go in for mathematics, which I could follow and learn and master, but in which I had no original power whatever. In other things, I could read French fairly well, from private reading; and I could read German almost as well. As for science, I knew nothing whatever about it. We only went through a little book of question and answer on political economy; we learned geography by making maps; if we learned history at all, I have forgotten in what way. We wrote an essay every week, which we had to divide and arrange in a certain fixed order—such as the Preface; the Reasoning; the Simile; the Quotation; the Illustration; the Argument; and the Conclusion. It was by this simple rule of thumb that the first lessons in arrangement and in construction were then taught, but I doubt if there could have been devised any better way of directing the mind unconsciously to obtain a sense of proportion and lucidity of arrangement. To this day, when I read an essay constructed loosely and confusedly I say, "My friend, you were never taught to divide your argument into those sections which make it more forcible and more attractive."

IV

King's College, London

King's College, London, where I was entered in October, 1854, was then even more than now considered as a bulwark of orthodoxy and the Established Church. To begin with, every student on admission was required to sign the Thirty-nine Articles. I believe the regulation was defended on the ground that, although a lad of seventeen was hardly likely to be a stalwart defender of these Articles, he acknowledged by signing them the principles of authority; he bowed before the teaching of his spiritual pastors, and accepted what he could neither prove nor disprove. Considering all that we have to accept on trust in the scientific world, perhaps it is not too much to invite this confidence on the part of a boy. Of course, all the Professors were Church of England men; there was a very terrible Council consisting of so many Grand Inquisitors; the least suspicion of heterodoxy was visited by deprivation. They were as implacable as the Holy Office. No reputation, no abilities, no services, no distinction could save the heretic. The orthodoxy of the College gave, however, no farther trouble to students than a weekly lecture by the Principal on these Articles which they had been made to accept on trust. During my year at the College we got through four, I remember—the first four. The remaining thirty-five I have continued to accept on trust.

I cannot say that the students were carefully looked after, or that the teaching could be called good. Our Professor of Classics, Dr. Browne, was a kindly and genial scholar. We translated a good deal. We wrestled with him all the time about learning Virgil by heart. He also gave us a course of Logic and another of Rhetoric, both of which, although very short and elementary, proved truly useful to one, at least, of his students. The Professor of Mathematics had been, I daresay, a good teacher in earlier years; when I joined he was old and had quite lost all interest in his work. Indeed, he no longer pretended any, but sat at his desk while the men worked at their own sweet will, bringing him from time to time difficulties and questions which he solved for them mechanically. There were French classes and German classes. There was a Greek Testament class, which I attended; it was compulsory.

Our best Professor was a man of considerable mark as an antiquary and archaeologist—the late J.S. Brewer. He was, if I remember right, Professor both of English History and of Literature, the two going together in those dark days. He was a stimulating lecturer, full of forcible eloquence and of enthusiasm for his subject. He could also on occasion show a rough side of tongue and temper.

So far as I can remember, there was very little in the way of social life among the students of my time. A Debating Society existed—I was a member, but never ventured to speak. I remember, however, the outrageous nonsense that was talked by the ingenuous youth—nonsense that set me against Debating Societies for life. I forget whether there were cricket and boat clubs, but I think not. There were a few residents, and I daresay they made a society of their own. Of the students who were there in my time one or two emerged afterwards from the ruck. Wace, afterwards Principal of King's, was one; a laborious scholar, who made the best use of his talents. I believe that he was for many years a leader writer for the *Times*. Ainger, at this moment Canon of Bristol and Master of the Temple, a man of accomplishments and readiness was another. Years afterwards I was present at the annual prize-giving. My former Professor, Archdeacon Browne, who had long before retired from his post, addressed the meeting. He said that it had afforded him peculiar gratification to observe the distinctions achieved by former students of King's. Among those who had thus risen to greatness, he said, were Bishops, Deans, Archdeacons, and Beneficed Clergy. No distinctions outside the Church were worth considering in a College so ecclesiastical, but the worthy Archdeacon represented the King's College of its founders.

I made a few friends in the college, some half dozen or so, who went on to Cambridge at the same time as myself. When lectures were over I used generally to walk away by myself into the City. There was no reason for getting into the City; I knew nothing about its history; but it fascinated me, as it does to this day. Apart from all its historical associations, the City has still a strange and inexplicable charm for me. I like now, as I liked then, to wander about among its winding lanes and narrow streets; to stand before those old, neglected City churchyards; to look into the old inn yards, of which there remain but one or two. If I could only by some effort of the memory recall those streets and houses, which I suppose I saw while they were still standing, but have forgotten! I knew the City before they provided it with the new broad thoroughfares; before they pulled down so many of the City churches. I ought to remember the double quadrangle of Doctors' Commons—that quaint old college in the heart of the City; Gerard's Hall; St. Michael's subterranean Church; the buildings on the site of the Hanseatic Aula; St. Paul's School; the Merchant Taylors' School; Whittington's Alms-House; and I know not what beside. Alas! I have long since forgotten them. In those days, however, I walked about among these ancient monuments. When I was tired and hungry I would look for a chop-house, dine, and then walk slowly home to my lodgings, taking a cup of coffee at a coffee-house on the way. My lodgings were in a place called Featherstone Buildings, Holborn. I shared rooms with a brother, who was in the City. He had a good many friends in London, and was out nearly every evening. I had few, and remained left to my own devices; we had little in common, and went each his own way; which is an excellent rule for brothers, and maintains fraternal affection.

I ought to have stayed at home in the evening and worked. Now Featherstone Buildings is a very quiet place; there is no thoroughfare; all the houses were then—and I daresay are still—let out in lodgings; our one sitting room, which was also my study, was the second floor front. In the evening the place was absolutely silent; the silence sometimes helped me in my work; sometimes it got on my nerves and became intolerable. I would then go out and wander about the streets for the sake of the animation, the crowds, and the lights; or I would go half-price—a shilling—to the pit of a theatre; or I would, also for a shilling, drop into a casino and sit in a corner and look on at the dancing. I was shy; I looked much younger than my age; I spoke to no one, and no one spoke to me. The thing was risky, but I came to no harm; nor did I ever think much about the character of the people who frequented the places. One of them was in Dean Street, Soho. It is now a school; it was then "Caldwell's"—a dancing place frequented by shop-girls, dressmakers, and young fellows. I do not know what the reputation of the place was; no doubt it was pretty bad; but, so far as I remember, it was a quiet and well-conducted place. To this day I cannot think of those lonely evenings in my London lodging without a touch of the old terror. I see myself sitting at a table, books spread out before me. I get to work. Presently I sit up and look round. The silence is too much for me. I take my hat and I go out. There are thousands of young fellows today who find, as I found every evening, the silence and loneliness intolerable. If I were a rich man I would build colleges for these young fellows, where they could live together, and so keep out of mischief. As for my friends, they were too far off to be of much use to me; they lived for the most part at Clapham and Camberwell, four miles away.

I have mentioned the brother who became Senior Wrangler. Two or three years afterwards he had a long and serious illness. At the same time my youngest sister—a child of six or so—was threatened with St. Vitus's Dance. As change of air was wanted for both, lodgings were taken at Freshwater Bay, in the Isle of Wight. I went with the two patients, and it was a delightful holiday. The sick people were convalescent. My brother talked to me all day long about Cambridge, and what he thought I ought to do. My imagination was fired. It seemed to me—it seems so still—the most splendid thing in the world for a young fellow to go to the University; there to contend with young giants; and, if he can, to keep his field and be victorious. My own victories proved humble, but I formed and cherished ambitions which were delightful, and at least I had the training.

I remember Freshwater for another reason. It was the beginning of the Crimean War, and Tennyson's *Maud* had just come out. I read the poem on the beach in that lovely bay; I saw the poet himself stalking among the hills—the Queen's Poet, the country people called him. I had seen the splendid fleets of which he spoke go forth to war. Heaven! How the lines at the end of Maud rang in my brain! The fleets went out to war, but they saw little; the war was carried on by the armies. In those days the poor lads had to face the awful Russian winter with brown paper boots, shoddy great-coats, and green coffee berries. I remember the people of Portsmouth going about with white faces, the men swearing and cursing, the women weeping. I remember, seeing the wounded borne on stretchers up the street to the new hospital under the walls. And I remember—saddest sight of all—seeing the remains of a regiment, that had been cut to pieces, marching from the Dockyard gates to the barracks—the band was reduced to five or six; the regiment was a skeleton. The men were ragged, and as they passed along they were followed by the weeping and wailing of the women. The poor degraded sailors' and soldiers' women had so much left of womanhood as to weep for the brave men who lay in the cemetery far away on the Crimean shores. I visited Freshwater again after forty years. Alas! the place is ruined. They have built a promenade round the little bay; there are rows of houses and villas and terraces. Tennyson's Freshwater is gone; no one would recognise, in the cockney watering-place, the lonely and secluded spot which furnished inspiration for Tennyson's most beautiful poem.

My three short terms at King's College, London, came to an end—not altogether ingloriously. I kept up the honour of my little school by taking the mathematical scholarship; I carried off prizes in classics, mathematics, and divinity. But nobody cared about any of the students; during the whole time I was there I never remember a single word of personal interest or of encouragement. The men went to lectures; if they failed to attend, a letter was sent to their people at home; of individual interest or encouragement there was absolutely none. I believe it was much the same thing at most of the colleges of Oxford and Cambridge at this time. The men were left severely alone; so that, after all, King's was not behind its betters.

One little distinction made me at the time very proud. It was in my first term. When the news came home of the Battle of the Alma, Trench, then Archbishop of Dublin, and formerly one of the professors of King's, sent a poem to the *Times* upon the victory. Professor Browne gave it to his class for Latin elegiacs. My copy, I was rejoiced to hear, was selected to be sent to the Archbishop. He wrote a very cordial letter in reply, with a kindly message to me. I wish I had kept the letter with that message.

One of my prizes, I have said, was for divinity. It was still my purpose to enter into holy orders. That is to say, I used to consider this my purpose. But as to any deliberate preparation for the life, or attempt to realise what it meant; or what was meant by the ecclesiastical mind; or to understand the necessity for acquiring the power of speaking, or of any qualification even distantly belonging to the clerical profession—I paid no attention and gave no thought to such things. Had I done so; had I realised the terrible weight of the fetters with which the average clergyman of the time went about laden—the chain of literal inspiration and verbal accuracy, the blind opposition to science, the dreary Evangelisations of the religious literature, the wrangles over points long since consigned to the limbo of old controversies, the intolerant spirit, the artificial life, the affected piety—I should have given up the thought of taking holy orders long before the decision was forced upon me.

During this period I began to write—or to make the first serious attempt at writing. That is to say, I had always been writing; as a boy, trying the most impossible things, even comedies. Now, however, I began to form definite ambitions. I would be a poet. I believe that this dream, which happens to thousands of lads of every degree, may be the most useful illusion possible. For it necessitates the writing of verse, and there is no kind of exercise more valuable, if one is destined to write prose, than the writing of verse, even though the result is by no means a success. My dream made me perfectly and entirely happy; my verses I thought splendid. Long years afterwards, when this youthful dream had been well-nigh forgotten, I came across a bundle of papers tied up carefully. They were my poems. Each was dated carefully, after the fashion of the bards of fame. I turned them over. Heavens! How could anyone, even in the present day, imagine or persuade himself that this stuff was poetry! I found crude and commonplace thoughts, echoes of Tennyson and Wordsworth—everything except what I had imagined when I wrote this skimble-skamble stuff. Suddenly I understood. The years rolled back. I saw myself with glowing cheek, with beating pulse, with humid eye, reading over what I had just written. And I saw that the young man read on the page before him, not the lame lines and the forced rhymes, but the thoughts in his own mind—the splendid thoughts, which were borrowed here and lifted there unconsciously, and which were lying in his brain waiting to be worked up and absorbed, and to form part of himself. And so this bundle of bad verses was in itself a part of education.

I once wrote a story—a very simple story it was—of three boys and a girl. One of my boys was a youth with literary ambitions. In my presentment of that youth I seem to see some kind of portrait, or sketch after the life, of myself. The book was called *All in a Garden Fair*, from which I have already quoted. Here is a passage in which the boy's early efforts are described:—

"'Such a boy as Allen is, before all things, fond of books. This means two things—first, that he is curious about the world, eager to learn, and, secondly, that he is open to the influences of form and style. Words and phrases move him in the silent page as the common man is moved by the orator. He has been seized by the charm of language. You understand me not, my daughter; but listen still. When a boy has once learned to love words, when he feels how a thing said one way is delightful, and said another way is intolerable, that boy may become a mere rhetorician, pedant, and precisian; or an orator, one of those who move the world; or a poet, one of those born to be loved.'

"'And Allen, you think, will be—what? A rhetorician, or an orator, or a poet?'

"'It may be the first, but I think he will not be. For I also observe in the boy the intuitions, the fire, the impatience, and the emotion, which belong to the orator who speaks because he must, and to the poet who writes because he cannot help it. I think—nay, I am sure—that a lad with these sympathies cannot be a mere rhetorician or a maker of phrases.'

"Claire listened, trying still to connect this theory with the conspiracy, but she failed.

"'He reads, because it is his time for reading everything. He has no choice. It is his nature to read. He was born to read. He reads by instinct. He reads poetry, and his brain is filled with magnificent colours and splendid women; he reads romances, and he dreams of knights and stately dames; he reads history, and his heart burns within him; he reads biography, and he worships great heroes; he reads tragedy, and he straightway stalks about the Forest another Talma; he reads idyls, and the meadows become peopled to him with the shepherds and shepherdesses—he lives two lives: one of these is dull and mean; to think of it, while he is living the other, makes him angry and ashamed, for in the other he lives in an enchanted world, where he is a magician and can conjure spirits.'"

I have not succeeded in becoming a poet; I still think, however, that there is nothing in the world so entirely desirable as a poetic life—if uninterrupted, without anxieties for the daily bread, sustained by noble thought, and encouraged by great success. Of all the men of our century I would rather have been Tennyson than any other man whatever.

However, I had my dream, and it was very delightful. And when I went up to Cambridge, exchanging my lonely lodgings in Holborn for a fuller and healthier social life, I ceased to think of poetry, and for three years almost ceased to think of writing at all. Once, I remember, I attempted a poem for the Chancellor's Prize. When I had half finished it, one of our men brought me a MS. It was his poem. No one was to be allowed to send in his composition in his own handwriting. Would I write it out for him? I looked at it with a sinking heart. It was a great deal better than mine. It was so unusually good that it failed to get the prize. Now mine was of a good honest mediocrity, so mediocre that I have often lamented the incident which prevented my sending it in.

V

CHRIST'S COLLEGE, CAMBRIDGE

I was entered at Christ's, one of the so called "small" colleges. It was then larger than most of the Oxford colleges, and stood about fifth on the list at Cambridge in point of numbers. All the colleges, however, in 1855 were much smaller than they are in 1900. Thus, our undergraduates were under a hundred in number; there are now at the same college two hundred.

I am strongly of opinion that a very large college, such as Trinity, Cambridge, does not offer anything like the social and educational advantages of a small college. Trinity, for instance, has about seven hundred undergraduates; Christ's, about two hundred. Now the chief advantage of a university course is the intercourse of the students among each other; the meeting of young men from all parts of the country and the Empire; the widening of views by free discussion. When there are only some fifty or sixty men of each year, they are drawn together by studies, by sports, by pursuits of all kinds; every man may make his mark upon his year; every man may get all that there is to be got by the society of other men of his own time. There are "sets," of course; a reading set; an athletic set; a musical set; a loafing set; a fast set. At Trinity, however, a man may be simply swamped. As it is, there is a tendency for the Eton men to keep together and make a set of their own; if a man does not belong to any of the great public schools, he will find it difficult to get into certain sets which may be intellectually the best; if he does not distinguish himself in any branch of learning, if he does not do well in athletics, if he shows no marked ability in any direction, it is quite possible for him to pass through Trinity as much neglected and alone as a solitary lodger in London. In a smaller college the sets overlap: it is realised that one may be a reading man and also an athlete. A freshman of ability is at once received into the best reading set; he gains the inestimable advantage for a young fellow of nineteen of knowing, and being influenced by, the third-year man who is about to distinguish himself in the Tripos, or even the Bachelor who has already distinguished himself. In the college of a hundred and fifty to two hundred men there is room for the development of character; no one need be lost in the crowd; the dullest of dull men may in some way or other make his mark and impress upon his contemporaries a sense of his individuality.

At other times and in other places I have advanced the theory that the eighteenth century did not really come to an end with December 31st, 1800, but that it lingered on until well into the nineteenth century, even to the beginning of Queen Victoria's eventful reign. In no place did it linger so long as at Cambridge. When I went up, the fellowships and the scholarships had been thrown open, but only recently, so that the Society was mainly composed of those who held close fellowships. These men, whose attainments had never been more than respectable, generally marked by a place somewhere among the wranglers, had for the most part come up from some small country town; they had a very faint tincture of culture; they were quite ignorant of modern literature; they knew absolutely nothing of art. As regards science, their contempt was as colossal as their ignorance. They vegetated at Cambridge; their lectures were elementary and contemptible; they lectured to freshmen on euclid, algebra or Greek Testament—the last for choice, because to fit them for the task they only had to read Bengel's *Gnomon* and other works of the kind, now perhaps—I don't know—forgotten; they divided the posts and offices of the college among themselves; they solemnly sat in the Combination Room for two hours everyday over their port; they sometimes played whist with each other; they hardly ever went outside the college except for an afternoon walk; and they waited patiently for a fat college living to fall in. When a vacancy happened, the next on the list took the place, went down, and was no more heard of.

The dulness, the incapacity, the stupidity of the dons brought the small colleges into a certain contempt. The decay of Cambridge as a place of learning threatened to overwhelm the university. I believe that for the first half of the century the scholarship and science of Cambridge were a laughing stock on the Continent. Naturally, the dulness of the fellows was in some sort reflected among the undergraduates. There were certain colleges which seemed never to show any intellectual life at all. I need not mention names, because everything is now changed. The close fellowship has now vanished; the close scholarship has been largely abolished; the entrance scholarships attract good men to the small as well as the large colleges; the fellows and lecturers of the former do not yield in intellectual attainments to those of the latter.

If the dons were different in the first half of the last century, how different were the undergraduates! In the fifties, the now universal habit of travel was unknown; the lads who came up to Cambridge had seen no other place than the small country town or country village from which they came. They were the sons of country gentlemen, but infinitely more rustic than their grandsons of the present day; they were the sons of the country clergy, well and gently bred, many of them, but profoundly ignorant of the world; they were the sons of manufacturers; they were the sons of professional men; they came from the country grammar school, which had not yet been converted into a public school after the one pattern now enforced; they had gone through the classical mill; they had learned a little mathematics; they played cricket with zeal; they were wholly ignorant of the world, of society, of literature, of everything. They mostly intended to take holy orders, and some of them had family livings waiting for them. It is difficult, in these days, to understand the depth, and the extent, and the intensity of the ignorance of these lads.

It happened, by great good luck for Christ's, that there had arisen a man in the college who had eyes to see and a head to understand. The man's name was Gunson; he was a Cumberland man, and prouder of being a "statesman" than of being tutor of his college. However, this man resolved upon converting his charge into a living and active seat of learning. First, he made his own lectures—classical lectures—worth attending; then, as there was no mathematician in the college, he got one of the ablest of the younger mathematicians in the university, Wolstenholme of St. John's, elected to a fellowship and lectureship at Christ's. Then he began to make things uncomfortable for the men who could read to good purpose and were idle. For the first time in the annals of the college there was seen a tutor who actually concerned himself about the men individually; who stormed and bullied the indolent and encouraged those who worked. The result was that, during the whole time that Gunson was tutor of Christ's, that is to say, for a quarter of a century, the college turned out a succession of men with whom no other college except Trinity could compare.

Let me enumerate some of the men who were members of the college during that quarter of a century when Gunson was tutor. It will be seen that some of them—the seniors—cannot be claimed as the results of Gunson's activity; but the great majority were undoubtedly his children.

To put the Church first, there were Frederick Gell, Bishop of Madras from 1861 to 1899; Sheepshanks, Bishop of Norwich; Sweatman, Bishop of Toronto; Henry Cheetham, Bishop of Sierra Leone; and Samuel Cheetham, Archdeacon of Rochester, and editor, with the late Sir William Smith, of the *Dictionary of Christian Antiquities*.—Among scholars, men of science, and men of other distinction, there were Sir John Robert Seeley, Professor of Modern History at Cambridge, author of the *Expansion of England*, and *Ecce Homo*; Charles Stuart Calverley, poet and scholar; Walter Skeat, Professor of Anglo-Saxon at Cambridge; John Peile, afterwards Master of Christ's College; J.W. Hales, Professor of English Literature at King's College, London; James Smith Reid, Professor of Ancient History; Walter Wren, the well-known coach; the Rev. C. Middleton-Wake, a writer on artistic topics; Dr. Robert Liveing, dermatologist; Sir Henry B. Buckley, Judge of the High Court; Sir Walter Joseph Sendall, G.C.M.G., Governor in turn of the Windward Islands, Barbados, Cyprus, and British Guiana; Sir John Jardine, K.C.I.E., Judge of the High Court of Bombay, and author of *Notes on Buddhist Law*; Richard Ebden, C.M.G., Chief Clerk at the Colonial Office; Sir Winfield Bonser, Chief Justice of Ceylon; S.H. Vynes, Professor of Botany at Oxford; H. Marshall Ward, Professor of Botany at Cambridge; George Henslow, also a famous botanist; A.E. Shipley, Lecturer on Morphology at Cambridge; Dr. Wallis Budge, the great Cuneiform scholar and keeper of the Egyptian and Assyrian Antiquities at the British Museum; and many others. I do not think that any other college except Trinity can show so goodly a list. To these may be added those who came to the college after taking their degree—Wolstenholme, third wrangler in 1850, my eldest brother's year, and late Professor of Mathematics at Cooper's Hill Engineering College; John Fletcher Moulton, K.C., Senior Wrangler and First Smith's Prizeman; Francis Darwin, author of *Practical Physiology of Plants*, and biographer of his distinguished father; and Robertson Smith, the man of colossal learning, Lord Almoner's Professor of Arabic at Cambridge, and joint editor of the *Encyclopædia Britannica*.

The greater number of these names belong to the late fifties and the early sixties. For my own part, I had the great good fortune of entering when Calverley had just taken his degree, when Seeley was a third year man; Skeat, Hales, Sendall, Peile belonged either to my own year or to that above or below. Seeley, as an undergraduate, was what he remained in after life, a leader and a teacher of men; he was always somewhat grave, even austere; always a student; always serious in his discourse and in his thoughts. To talk daily with him was an education. He was most helpful to younger men in whom he took an interest; for my own part, I have to thank him for opening up a new world to me. My opportunities of conversation with scholars had been few. At school there had been none; my head-master never talked to the boys; at King's College there had been none, the professors and lecturers paid no attention to the students. I had read voraciously, but not always wisely. Seeley introduced me to Carlyle, Maurice and Coleridge. Without intending it, he made it impossible for me to carry out my original purpose of taking holy orders. That is to say, the teaching of Maurice, acting on a mind very little attracted by the prevalent orthodoxy, which was still Calvinist and Evangelical, caused a gradual revolt, which was quite unconscious until the time came when I was forced to contemplate the situation seriously. This, however, came afterwards.

Among these men—I mean of my own time—incomparably the most brilliant, the finest scholar, the most remarkable man from every point of view, was Calverley. He was the hero of a hundred tales; all the audacious things, all the witty things, all the clever things, were fathered upon him. It is forty years since his time, and no doubt the same audacities, repartees, and things of unexpectedness which never die have been fathered upon others, his successors in brilliant talk and scholarship. But consider, to a lad like myself, the delight of knowing a man who was not only the finest scholar of his year—writing Latin verses which even to eyes like mine were charming—but a man who could play and sing with a grace and sweetness quite divine, as it seemed to me; who could make parodies the most ridiculous and burlesques the most absurd; who kept a kind of open house for his intimates, with abundance of port and claret—he was the only man in college who kept claret; whose English verses were as delightful as his Latin; who was always sympathetic, always helpful, always considerate. In my first year I saw very little of him. That was to be expected, considering that he was already a bachelor. But a fortunate accident caused him to become then and thenceforward one of my best and kindest friends. The occasion was this. The college offered, every year, a gold medal for an English Essay; the prize was provided by Bishop Porteous, one of the Christ's worthies. I sent in an essay, and to my surprise, I obtained the prize. More than this, I was bracketed with Calverley. For a freshman of nineteen to be bracketed equal in an English essay with the most brilliant scholar of his time was too much to be expected. I have never since experienced half the joy at any success which I felt on that occasion. Needless to say that I have kept the medal ever since in remembrance of that bracket.

My university career was creditable but not greatly distinguished. I read for double honours, but only went out in the Mathematical Tripos. My classical reading, however, was not wasted, because you cannot well waste time in reading Latin and Greek. I was a scholar, an exhibitioner and a prizeman of my college; I obtained a place tolerably high among the wranglers of my year. My friends groaned, and said I ought to have done much better. Perhaps, but then I had done very much better than they imagined in the broadening of my views, and in general knowledge and culture. I completed my course at Christ's, as I had begun it, by taking a special prize—this time the Bachelor's Theological Prize.

The undergraduate's life in the fifties differed in many respects from that of his successor in the nineties. To begin with, there was a far more generous consumption of beer. Many reading men began the day with beer after breakfast; every Sunday morning breakfast was concluded with beer; there was more beer for lunch; nothing but beer was taken with dinner; and there was beer with the evening pipe. Every college had its own brewer. Four kinds of beer were brewed: the "Audit" ale, old and strong, the "Strong" ale, the "Bitter," and the "Small" beer, or "Swipes"; the common dinner drink was "Bitter and Swipes." We dined at four—a most ungodly hour, maintained in the belief that it would leave a long evening for work; it left a long evening, it is true, but not much of it was spent in work. Everyday after hall the men divided themselves into little parties of four or six, and took wine in each other's rooms; with the reading men there was not much taken, one bottle of port generally sufficing for the whole of the little company. Chapel broke up the party at six. Tea was generally taken at seven or thereabouts, when work was supposed to be resumed and carried on as long as each man chose; mostly at about ten books were laid aside, pipes were produced, and with a quart of bitter for the two or three gathered together, the day was ended before midnight.

Lectures went on from nine to eleven; there was the private coach every other day from eleven to one or two; a hasty lunch of bread and cheese and beer, or of bread and butter with a glass of sherry, followed; then the river, or racquets, or fives, or a walk till four. This was our life. My own form of exercise was either boating or fives. I went down to the river almost every afternoon, rowing bow in our first boat, which was not very high—ninth, I think. In the long vacation, when the narrow river was clearer, I went sculling a good deal. I also played fives, the only game of ball which I could play, because it was the only game in which I could see the ball.

A few men belonged to the Union, but not many. There was no amalgamated club subscription; the cricket club and the boating club were the only two which asked for subscriptions. There were no athletics to speak of; the university sports were held on Fenner's Ground, but not many men took part in them, or even went to look on. There was no football club for the college; there were no musical societies; there was no choir in the Chapel; there were no associations among the undergraduates at all except two whist clubs. The "muckle" pewter belonging to one of these clubs still adorns my study. In some colleges they had supper clubs, which meant spending a great deal more than the men could afford, and drinking a great deal more than was good for them. I do not think that any supper club existed at Christ's in my time.

On Sunday after Chapel, *i.e.* about half-past ten, there was always a breakfast of some half-dozen men; the breakfast consisted of a solid cold pie and the usual "trimmings," with beer afterwards. After breakfast we went for a long walk. Cambridge is surrounded by villages with venerable churches. They are separated, it is true, by three or four miles of flat and treeless country, but, in the course of a morning between eleven and four, one could cover a good stretch of ground. In those days the rustics still wore embroidered smocks on Sunday and the women wore scarlet flannel shawls. Those of the undergraduates who were religiously disposed indulged in a sort of gluttonous banquet of services. One man, I remember, would take a Sunday school at eight A.M., go to chapel at half-past nine; to a morning service at eleven; to the university sermon at two; to King's College Chapel at three; to the college chapel at six; to evening service in some church of the town at seven, and end with a prayer meeting and hymn singing in somebody's rooms. But such men were rare. For my own part, though still proposing to take orders, I was so little moved by the responsibilities before me that though it was necessary, in order to obtain the proper college testimonials, to attend three celebrations of Holy Communion in the three years of residence, I forgot this requirement, and, on discovering the omission, attended all three in the last two terms. This was thought somewhat scandalous, and I nearly lost my college certificate in consequence.

As for the literary tastes of my times, Tennyson, Kingsley and Carlyle were in everybody's hands, with Dickens of course as the first favourite.

It is wonderful that no one seems to have heard of Robert Browning, but I am quite certain that I read nothing of Browning until after going down. Yet we knew, and read, Wordsworth, Keats, Coleridge, Byron, Scott—in a word, all the poets. Another omission is Thackeray. I cannot remember when I first read *Vanity Fair* and the smaller things; but I fear that they did not impress me, as they should have done, with anything like the true sense of the writer's greatness. It must be remembered that literary circles were then very few and very limited. We were most of us country lads, who were still reading the literature of the past. To us, it was more important to study Shakespeare, Milton, Dryden, Pope, Addison, Fielding and the other great writers who were gone, than to be inquiring about Thackeray's last work. We knew nothing and cared nothing about the literary gossip of the time; we made no inquiries about the literary men of the day; some of the men read Evangelical books; most read nothing at all; a few, as I have said, tried to get some mastery over English literature as a continuous development—but they were very few. The ignorance and the apathy of the great mass of men at Cambridge as regards literature was amazing. The best scholars in Greek and Latin only regarded English poetry as a medium to be rendered into Greek Iambics or Latin Lyrics; the mathematicians, as a rule, knew and cared for nothing outside their mathematics.

As for the profession of letters, that, in any shape, was regarded with pity and contempt. The late Tom Taylor, sometime Fellow of Trinity and afterwards dramatist, man of letters, and editor of *Punch*, was always spoken of by his old friend, the tutor of Christ's, as "poor Tom Taylor!" Yet "poor Tom" did very well; made a little noise in his own day; lived in plenty and comfort; and among literary folk was well regarded. The literary life, however, was still languishing in contempt. Writers by profession were many of them hacks, dependents, Bohemians, and disreputable in their manners. So, at least, they were regarded; and, if one reads about the writers of the forties and the fifties, not without some reason.

The only journalism that was accounted worthy of a gentleman and a scholar was the writing of leaders for the *Times*. When the penny newspapers began, great was the derision heaped upon the "young lions" by their contemporaries who started the *Saturday Review*. The university, in fact, considered only two professions: the Church, which included lectureships, professorships, and fellowships at the colleges; and the Bar. Nothing else was thought worthy of a scholar. Schoolmastering was a refuge, not a profession; art was an unknown calling—to the university; the other professions, as architecture, the work of the actuary, engineering, science of all kinds, were not recognised. They belonged, perhaps, to University College, London, and the current and kindly name for that institution was "Stinkomalee."

I have mentioned the *Saturday Review*. That paper first appeared in my undergraduate days, and did more to create journalism as a profession than would be believed at the present moment, when journalists are recruited from all classes. It was understood, at the outset, that it was wholly written by university men, and mostly by Cambridge men; their names were whispered—the names of dons. The paper assumed the manner of authority; such authority as a scholar has a right to exercise; that is to say, a superior manner, as of deeper and wider knowledge. It heaped derision on the shams of the time; and especially on the shams which had gathered round the Evangelical party; the pietistic sermons; the snuffling hypocrisies; the half-concealed, self-seeking, the narrowness, and the tyranny of it; the scamped services and the wretched buildings and villainous singing. Never was a party more handsomely banged and beaten week after week; never was derision more piled up with every number than over the cant and the unreality of this party. On Sunday the paper became part of the breakfast; it was read with a savage joy. I think, looking back, that the slating and the bludgeoning were quite too savage; yet the fearlessness with which the bludgeon or the rapier was handled impressed the world. None of the Evangelical lights were spared. Lord Shaftesbury heard, to his disgust, that his deity was an old man of an uncertain temper sitting on a cloud; a great light in the Evangelical party was shown by his own recorded prayers before going into the Senate House to have treated the Almighty as a judicious coach; the early extravagances of Charles Spurgeon, then regarded in certain circles as another Wesley, were exposed; the missionaries of the narrow school were handled with a dexterity which Sydney Smith might have envied. The excuse for this savagery was that the time wanted it. I do not think that a paper conducted on the same lines would now do any good at all; but we want now, and want it badly, a paper written wholly by scholars who will speak with the authority of scholars. The *Saturday Review* began to fall off when it began to lose its old authority.

There was no ladies' society, or very little, at Cambridge. I myself was so fortunate as to be invited to one or two houses where there were daughters. Most of the men had no chance of speaking to a lady during the whole of the university course. Many of our men came from country farms, or were drawn from the "statesmen" of Cumberland; you may imagine, therefore, that they were tolerably rough. The three years of Cambridge did something for them, but there were no compensations for the loss of ladies' society. None of the dons were married; the heads of houses and the professors alone were married. As for the town, I do not think that there was any kind of intercourse between the town of Cambridge and the colleges.

The university, in fact, was still a collection of monastic establishments. It was the end of a sleepy time, but change was rapidly approaching. I saw the place, I repeat, as it had been all through the eighteenth century. With the men of my time I felt the coming change. Close fellowships were thrown open; close scholarships fell into the common treasury of endowment; science was beginning to demand recognition; scholars were looking across to Germany with envy; the rule of the Evangelicals was relaxing. Dissenters and Jews were beginning to be admitted to the university. They had to go to chapel and to pass the "little go," with its examination upon Paley's *Evidences of Christianity*; and they could hold neither fellowship nor scholarship. They were allowed, however, to go in for the Tripos examinations.

I have omitted to allude to one little distinction that I gained. In my second year, Calverley announced an examination for a prize in the study of the *Pickwick Papers*. The examination was held in the evening in his own rooms. If I remember aright there were about ten candidates, most of whom had no chance whatever. The paper, a copy of which is appended, is one of the cleverest things that Calverley ever did. We were allowed, I think, two hours, or perhaps three. When the papers were handed in, we refreshed ourselves after our labours with a supper of oysters, beer, and milk-punch. The result gave me the first prize, and Skeat the second. There was a good deal of talk about the examination; copies of the paper were in great request all over the university; and for a whole day Skeat and I were famous.

Another little episode. One day Calverley, then a fellow, stopped me in the court and invited me to his rooms after hall. "I 've got a young Frenchman," he said. "He's clever. Come and be amused." I went. The young Frenchman spoke English as well as anybody; he told quantities of stories in a quiet, irresponsible way, as if he was an outsider looking on at the world. No one went to chapel that evening. After the port, which went round with briskness for two or three hours, the young Frenchman went to the piano and began to sing in a sweet, flexible, high baritone or tenor. Presently somebody else took his place at the instrument, and he, with Calverley, and two or three dummies, performed a Royal Italian Opera in very fine style. The young Frenchman's name was George Du Maurier. Years afterwards, when I came to know him, I reminded him of this blissful evening—which he remembered perfectly. One of the songs he sang in French had a very sweet and touching air. Calverley remembered it, and Sendall wrote some verses for it. They are preserved as a footnote to some reminiscences of mine in Sendall's memoir of Calverley, his brother-in-law.

And so my time came to an end. What did Cambridge do for me? Well, it seems as if it did everything for me. For a time, at least, it knocked on the head all my literary aspirations. As regards literature, indeed, I understood that I had to study the poets of my own speech seriously, and I began to do so. Writing had to wait. It made holy orders impossible for me, though, as yet, I did not understand this important fact. It widened the whole of my mind in every imaginable way. It seems to me now, looking back, that except for my three early years with H. A——, my education only began when I entered college; imperfect as it was when I left, I had, at least, acquired standards and models. I was reputed, I believe, to have failed in my degree. Well, there are so many other useful things besides mathematics, and I was quite high enough for any mathematical powers that I possessed. I had obtained, in addition, much Latin and Greek, and a certain insight into Divinity, with a good solid foundation of English, French, and German literature, read by myself. There is another point. Much more in those days than at present, when everything is levelled, was Cambridge a school of manners. Consider: we were all thrown together in a small college, on terms of intimacy. There was, as I have said, the son of the country gentleman of good family; the son of the country clergyman; the son of the London merchant; the son of the London physician, barrister, or solicitor; the lad from the country town; the lad from the farm; the lad from the manufacturing centre; the son of the tradesman: all these lads lived together in amity. But there were leaders among us, and manners were softened—things were learned which had not been guessed before. New habits of thought, new points of refinement, a wider mind, came out of this intimacy of so many different youths from different homes. If I may

WALTER BESANT

judge from myself, the effect of Cambridge upon the youth of the time was wholly and unreservedly beneficial.

AN EXAMINATION PAPER.
"THE POSTHUMOUS PAPERS OF THE PICKWICK CLUB."
CAMBRIDGE (1857)

1. Mention any occasions on which it is specified that the Fat Boy was *not* asleep; and that (1) Mr. Pickwick and (2) Mr. Weller, senior, ran. Deduce from expressions used on one occasion Mr. Pickwick's maximum of speed.

2. Translate into coherent English, adding a note wherever a word, a construction, or an allusion, requires it:—

   "Go on, Jemmy—like black-eyed Susan—all in the Downs"—"Smart chap that cabman—handled his fives well—but if I'd been your friend in the green jemmy—punch his head—pig's whisper—pieman, too."

   Elucidate the expression, "the Spanish Traveller," and the "narcotic bedstead."

3. Who were Mr. Staple, Goodwin, Mr. Brooks, Villam, Mrs. Bunkin, "Old Nobs," "cast-iron head," "young Bantam?"

4. What operation was performed on Tom Smart's chair? Who little thinks that in which pocket, of what garment, in where, he has left what, entreating him to return to whom, with how many what, and all how big?

5. Give, approximately, the height of Mr. Dubbley; and, accurately, the Christian names of Mr. Grummer, Mrs. Raddle, and the Fat Boy; also the surname of the Zephyr.

6. "Mr. Weller's knowledge of London was extensive and peculiar." Illustrate this by a reference to the facts.

7. Describe the Rebellion which had irritated Mr. Nupkins on the day of Mr. Pickwick's arrest?

8. Give in full Samuel Weller's first compliment to Mary, and his father's critique upon the same young lady. What church was on the valentine that first attracted Mr. Samuel's eye in the shop?

9. Describe the common Profeel-machine.

10. State the component parts of dog's nose; and simplify the expression "taking a grinder."

11. On finding his principal in the pound, Mr. Weller and the town-beadle varied directly. Show that the latter was ultimately eliminated, and state the number of rounds in the square which is not described.

12. "Any think for air and exercise; as the wery old donkey observed ven they voke him up from his deathbed to carry ten gen'lmen to Greenwich in a tax-cart." Illustrate this by stating any remark recorded in the Pickwick Papers to have been made by a (previously) dumb animal, with the circumstances under which he made it.

13. What kind of cigars did Mr. Ben Allen chiefly smoke, and where did he knock and take naps alternately, under the impression that it was his home?

14. What was the ordinary occupation of Mr. Sawyer's boy? whence did Mr. Allen derive the idea that there was a special destiny between Mr. S. and Arabella?

15. Describe Weller's Method of "gently indicating his presence" to the young lady in the garden; and the form of salutation usual among the coachmen of the period.

16. State any incidents you know in the career of Tom Martin, butcher, previous to his incarceration.

17. Give Weller's Theories for the extraction of Mr. Pickwick from the Fleet. Where was his wife's will found?

18. How did the old lady make a memorandum, and of what, at whist? Show that there were at least three times as many fiddles as harps in Muggleton at the time of the ball at Manor Farm.

19. What is a red-faced Nixon?

20. Write down the chorus to each verse of Mr. S. Weller's song, and a sketch of the mottle-faced man's excursus on it. Is there any ground for conjecturing that he (Sam) had more brothers than one?

21. How many lumps of sugar went into the Shepherd's liquor as a rule? and is any exception recorded?

22. What seal was on Mr. Winkle's letter to his father? What penitential attitude did he assume before Mr. Pickwick?

23. "She's a-swelling visibly." When did the same phenomenon occur again, and what fluid caused the pressure on the body in the latter case?

24. How did Mr. Weller, senior, define the Funds, and what view did he take of Reduced Consols? in what terms is his elastic force described, when he assaulted Mr. Stiggins at the meeting? Write down the name of the meeting?

25. Προβατογνώμων: a good judge of cattle; hence, a good judge of character. Note on Æsch. Ag.—Illustrate the theory involved by a remark of the parent Weller.

26. Give some account of the word "fanteeg," and hazard any conjecture explanatory of the expression "My Prooshan Blue," applied by Mr. Samuel to Mr. Tony Weller.

27. In developing to P.M. his views of a proposition, what assumption did Mr. Pickwick feel justified in making?

28. Deduce from a remark of Mr. Weller, junior, the price per mile of cabs at the period.

29. What do you know of the hotel next the Bull at Rochester?

30. Who, besides Mr. Pickwick, is recorded to have worn gaiters?

VI

A Tramp Abroad

To some it may be astonishing to find young men eager to get through their university course in order to get back to the old school in which they want to work for the whole of their lives. Yet there is no kind of work more delightful to those who are born for it than that of a master in a public school. Anyone with ordinary powers of insight and sympathy can teach a pupil willing to be taught. The work of the schoolmaster is more than to teach the willing; it is to convert the unwilling into the willing; to make the indolent active, to stimulate the flagging, and to watch over every boy under his care. There are the pleasures of authority and power for him; he is an unquestioned dictator; he is a judge; he awards punishments and prizes. It is not a line that makes many demands upon the intellect. Most schoolmasters never advance beyond the routine of their daily work; the mathematician forgets the higher mathematics; the chemist ceases his research; the scholar works no more at his subjects; all are content with the knowledge that they have acquired, and with the equipment that is wanted for the day's work.

On the other hand, to one who is not born for that kind of work the position is by no means pleasant, and to some it is intolerable. In my own case it was not pleasant, but it was not intolerable. After a few months of looking about and waiting, during which I made certain first attempts at journalism, I took a mastership in a school. The school was Leamington College, and I was chosen as mathematical master, with the understanding that I was to be ordained and to become, in addition, chaplain to the college. The head-master at the time was the Rev. E. St. John Parry, a good scholar and, I think, a good schoolmaster. The town was full of pleasant people. Some of them were hospitable to me, and I have very friendly recollections of the place. The boys belonged chiefly to the higher class in the town. I formed an alliance with another master. We took a small house and made ourselves comfortable; the hours were by no means long, and we were not, as is the case with many schools, surrounded by boys all day and every evening.

While at Leamington I had a great experience. I have said that in those days very few of the undergraduates knew anything about foreign travel. In my own case, for instance, at twenty-three years of age what had I seen? I had never been abroad at all. Of England I had seen London, Cambridge, Ely, Winchester, Liverpool, my native town, and the Isle of Wight. It seems to a modern young man who runs about everywhere, and is more familiar with Cairo than with Cheapside, a poor show. Mine, however, was not by any means an exceptional case. The younger dons had begun to travel: in the famous tour—is it still famous?—of "Brown, Jones, and Robinson," one at least of the three was a Cambridge man. They took reading parties to the Lakes and into Scotland—is Clough's poem, his long-vacation pastoral, "The Bothie of Tober-na-Vuolich" still remembered? They went about with knapsacks, just as the young fellows with bicycles now go about, but they walked. And they had begun the craze for Alpine climbing, which is still with us, somewhat moderated. It was the beginning of athletics. The men who trudged with the knapsacks were called "Mussulmen"—a subtle and crafty joke.

It was with the greatest joy that I received a proposal to join Calverley and Peile on a walking tour. They proposed to try the Tyrol, then off the beaten track, with no modern hotels and little or no experience of tourists. With us was Samuel Walton, a Fellow of St. John's, one of the first of those who braved the world and wore a beard. He was also one of the most kindly and amiable of creatures; well read, sympathetic, always in good temper, and the best travelling companion possible. He became afterwards Rector of Fulbourne, and died at two-and-thirty of consumption.

It was arranged that I should join Walton at Heidelberg, where he had been learning German for three or four months; that we were to go on to Innsbruck, where Calverley and Peile would join us, and that then the knapsack business would begin. I carried with me a flannel suit, which at the outset looked quite nice and cool; I wore a pair of stout boots studded with nails for walking on ice; in my knapsack I had a spare shirt, a nightshirt, another collar, a brush and comb, socks, handkerchiefs, toothbrush, pipe and tobacco. I had no change of clothes, and my flannels were a light grey in colour. Thus equipped I started for a six weeks' journey. The other men were as lightly clad and as slenderly provided.

It was all perfectly delightful. I believe, but I am not sure, that I went through by way of Ostend to Cologne, a journey then of about twenty-four hours. From Cologne I got to Königswinter, saw the Drachenfels, and went up the Rhine. I remember that there was a delightful American family on board the boat. I made my way to Heidelberg, and I found Walton waiting for me. The other day I was at Heidelberg again, and I tried to find the place where we stayed, but failed. It was a lodging, not a hotel, and we took our meals at a students' restaurant, where things were cheap and plentiful, and where the wine was of a thinness and sourness inconceivable to one whose ideas of wine were based on port and sherry. We saw the students marching about in their flat caps, with shawls over their shoulders; we saw them in their beer-drinking, and we saw them at a duel with swords—one is glad to have seen so much. We wandered over the castle—there was no inclined railway up the hill in those days; we bathed in the Neckar, ice-cold and swift; we climbed the opposite hill and discovered another castle. We talked German religiously—there were maidens at our lodgings, who made it pleasant to learn their language. I had read a good deal of German at school and afterwards, so that I had a foundation in grammar and vocabulary. One wants very little grammar to get along in German, and to understand it. It is the vocabulary that is wanted. By dint of finding out the names of everything in German, I made rapid progress in a helter-skelter way. I was sorry to leave Heidelberg, and should have been content to give up the mountains and the glaciers, and to complete my German studies in this very pleasant manner.

However, we had to go. I forget the geography; we went on to Innsbruck, somehow. I remember that we passed a lovely lake, called, I think, the Aachen See; that we stopped at a fashionable hotel filled with Germans; and that we took two or three preliminary climbs in the hills. However, we got to Innsbruck; and while we waited for the other two, we climbed a big rolling mountain, not a peak, close to the ancient town. Then the other two men came and we began our march.

Where did we go? I don't know. Down the Zeller Thal, where they sang to us in the evening, and we sang to them. Calverley had a pleasing tenor, Walton an excellent bass, and my voice, though of poor quality, was tolerably high. We sang the old glees, "All among the Barley"; "Cares that Canker"; "Hark! the Lark"; and so on. The Tyrolese were good enough to applaud. They were, I remember, extremely friendly.

Then we came to a mountain—was it the Gross Glockner?—which we proposed to climb. Heavens! How high it looked! and how steep were the sides! I, for one, was delighted, I confess, when our guides came and said that the mountain was too dangerous; that there had been so much rain that the snow slopes were not safe; in a word, they would not take us.

So we wandered elsewhere. I remember getting to a hut high on a mountain side; they gave us something to eat; we slept on straw; in the morning we started at half past four with a breakfast of fried eggs and coarse bread and melted snow. We had before us a "low pass." We should get to our halting place at four or five in the afternoon. Unfortunately, we took a wrong line and crossed a high pass, not a low pass. We had no food of any kind with us; only a single flask with schnaps; it was the hardest day's work I had ever done. Finally we got to our inn at half past eight in the evening. They gave us veal cutlets and bread; and after supper, I, for my part, lay down on the floor and slept till eight next morning.

It was a glorious time, but the days passed all too quickly. At Meran I had to leave the party and get home as fast as I could. The flannel suit was a sight to behold. Cruel thorns had lacerated the skirts, rains had fallen upon it, discolouration disfigured it, and I had to get through Switzerland and France in the most disreputable rig possible to imagine. Part of my journey was a night spent in a diligence. My fellow passengers were two nuns, or sisters. One of them was elderly, the other was young, and we talked the whole night through. They asked endless questions about England. We were not tired or sleepy in the least; and when we parted it was like the parting of old friends. My very dear ladies, I cherish the memory of that night. It was all too short.

I remember stopping at a fashionable hotel in Zurich, where I took an obscure corner and hoped to escape observation. I arrived in Paris with a five-pound note and a few coppers at half-past five or six in the morning. What was I to do? I found a restaurant and a waiter, looking very sleepy, sweeping out the place. I told him that I wanted change, and showed him the note. He took me to a den up ever so many stairs, where sat an Englishman of villainous aspect. He gave me a handful of French money, which he said was the equivalent of the note, less his commission. I daresay he was a perfectly honest man, but I could never understand how it was that, after taking breakfast at my restaurant and travelling second class by Dieppe to Portsmouth, I had only fourpence left out of my five-pound note.

I came back to Leamington to find trouble brewing. The governors of the college wanted to know when I was going to be ordained. By this time I had passed the voluntary theological examination at Cambridge, and had nothing more to do except to pass the Bishop's examination. I put myself in communication with the Bishop's secretary, and with great depression of spirits prepared myself for perjury, because by this time I understood that the white tie would choke me.

Then I heard that there were rumours among the governors. Somebody said that he feared—he was told—it was rumoured—that I was not sound on the Atonement. And day by day the truth was borne in upon me that I was not called and chosen for the office of deacon in the Church of England.

Christmas came. I was to be ordained in the spring; the Bishop had my name; my credentials had been sent to him. And then—oh! happiness!—a door of release was thrown open. My friend Ebden, then a junior in the Colonial College, came to see me. In his hand, so to speak, he held two colonial professorships. It seemed not improbable that I might have either of them if I chose. Then I should not have to take orders; then I should see something more of the world; then I should travel across the ocean. If I chose? Of course I chose. I jumped at the chance. I sent in my name. I was appointed. My choice was for the Mauritius, because the other place was in South Africa, and I don't like snakes. So when I returned to Leamington it was to give in my resignation in three months, with the joy of feeling that I need not trouble the Bishop of Worcester—to whom I forgot to send an excuse—and that no one thenceforward would so much as ask whether I was sound on the Atonement.

It was a plunge; it was an escape. Whither I was going, what adventures I should meet with, how things would end, I knew not, nor did I ask myself. Why should one pry into the future? Though I could not suspect the fact, I was about to equip myself—with travel, with the society of all kinds of men, with the acquisition of things practical—for the real solid work of my life, which has been the observation of men and women, and the telling of stories about them.

VII

L'Île de France

It was before the time of the Suez Canal, and before the time of big liners. The ship that carried me to Alexandria was called one of the finest in the fleet of the Peninsular and Oriental Company. She was a paddle-wheel of twelve hundred tons, named the *Indus*. It was before the time of competitive companies. The P. and O. managed things their own way; their rates were high, but they treated the passengers like guests in a country house. There was no drinking on board, but at lunch and dinner bottled beer and wine were put on the table, as at a gentleman's house. After dinner the wine remained on the table for a short time; in the evening whiskey and brandy were put out for half an hour only. A band was on board, which played every afternoon; the passengers danced on deck; the ship ploughed her way slowly through the waters; in the cabins all lights were out at nine—or ten—I forget which. As a junior, I had a bunk in a cabin below the main deck. There were five berths assigned to young fellows going out to India; the place was dark at mid-day, and at night the darkness was Egyptian. The weather, however, was fine, and one was on deck from early morning till nightfall, and one was young, and small discomforts mattered nothing. Besides, were we not seeing the world?

I seem to remember everyday of that voyage; the coast of Portugal; the headlands of Spain; the Rock; Malta, where we all went ashore and saw the town of Valetta, the Cathedral, and the Palace of the Knights.

We landed at Alexandria and went on by train to Cairo, where we stayed, I think, two nights, and saw an eastern city—it was really eastern then.

Then we went on by a shaky railway across the desert to Suez. It was a great joy actually to see the rolling grey sand of the desert. Half way over we stopped at a desert station, where they gave us luncheon. Then we got to Suez, and here we divided. The passengers for Mauritius and Réunion went on board their little boat, and the Bombay people went on board their big boat.

Our boat, in fact, was a little steamer of seven hundred tons, quite unfit for bad weather. Fortunately we had none. But it was in May, and the Red Sea was beginning to assert itself. In the cabins the heat was stifling; and they were infested with flying cockroaches and other creatures of prey. Therefore the whole company slept on deck. The mattresses were lugged up and spread out, and we lay side by side, with faces muffled to keep off the moonshine. It was curious to wake in the night and to see by the light of the moon the sleeping figures, and to watch the waves in the white light, and the jagged outline of the mountains of Arabia. In the evening, when we were near enough to see them, the rocks assumed all colours, purple, blue, crimson, golden. Among them the mountain they call Sinai reared its rugged head, painted by the western glow.

We put in at Aden, and saw the native village and the water-works. Then we coasted round the rockbound Socotra and steered south for the Seychelles. I suppose there are other islands in the world as beautiful as these, but I have seen none that could approach them for the wonderful magic of the hills, which slope down to the water's edge, covered with trees and clothed in colour. The hot sun of the tropics, that knows no change, and has no season but one, makes a long summer of the year; the sea that washes the feet of the hills is aglow with a warm light that makes it transparent; fathoms below the ship one could see the tangled forest of weed lying still and motionless; above the weed rolled slowly an enormous shark.

I believe the islanders have no energy; no ambitions are left to them after a year or two in the place; they have no desire for wealth; they leave nature to grow a few things for them to send away; they want very little money; they care nothing for the outside world; they lie in the shade, warmed through and through; the air is never scorching and the heat never kills, for there is always a sea breeze, cool and sweet, morning and evening. There is a resident Commissioner, who has nothing to do; there is a magistrate; there are one or two priests. There was an Anglican missionary, but in such a climate no one troubles to think about religion, no one wants a change; life comes unasked, it lasts awhile, it goes away. Where does it go? Nobody asks; nobody cares. On the verandah one sits with feet up and looks out into the forest beyond the bananas and the palms. Life *is*. What more does one want? Why should one inquire?

From Seychelles, a run of some 1,500 miles brings us to Mauritius. It is forty years since I landed at Port Louis. I believe there have been great changes. In 1867 a malarious fever declared itself, which has been endemic ever since. Port Louis was a gay and a sociable place in 1861. The wealthy quarter contained large and handsome houses, with gardens and deep verandahs. There was an open "Place," where the band played in the afternoon, while the carriages went round and round. There was a great deal of dinner giving; there were dances in the cool season; there was an Opera House, maintained by subscription; there were two regiments in the place, besides artillery and engineers. What was more important to me was that I arrived at a time when everybody was young. In such a colony the merchants and planters in the good old times got rich and went home, leaving their affairs in the hands of younger men. It so happened that the houses of business were at this time nearly all in the hands of the younger men, consequently they were lively. Moreover, a railway was about to be constructed, and we received a large addition to the Englishmen by the arrival of the engineers who were to construct it.

In this place, then, I lived for six years and a half. There was a good deal of monotony, but the general tone was one of great cheerfulness. After a while I found the air of Port Louis, which is surrounded by an amphitheatre of hills from 1,200 to 2,500 feet high, confined and relaxing. I therefore joined a mess of bachelors and lived for a time three or four miles out. We had a series of changes, for the men in the mess came and went. They were railway engineers; they were Civil servants; they were managers and accountants of the banks; they were partners in mercantile houses. Finally, and for the last two years, I settled in a charming little bungalow ten miles from town, with a garden growing most of the English and all the tropical vegetables, a mountain stream at the back, and a pool for bathing, and within reach of the central forests.

As regards the college, I would say as little as possible, because it was a time of continual fight between the rector and the professors. The former is now dead, but probably there are living those who would be hurt by certain reminiscences. Suffice it to say, therefore, that he was a very clever and able man in the wrong place. He had been in the Austrian army, and retained a good deal of the Austrian ideas as to duty and discipline, which did not suit either an English public school, such as the Government, which kept up the college at a heavy loss, desired, or a French *lycée*, which it was, to all intents and purposes. He spoke French and English fluently, but both with a strong German accent, which made him look ridiculous; he was not a scholar in any sense of the word; he knew nothing that I could ever discover—certainly neither Latin, nor Greek, nor mathematics, nor history. His only notions of teaching were those of an army crammer; as for subjects to be taught, or text-books to be used, he knew absolutely nothing. His fitness for the post is illustrated by the fact that he wanted English history to be studied by young men of nineteen or twenty out of a miserable little book compiled for candidates for German cavalry and infantry! I do not know who was responsible for sending the poor man to the place; but imagine the wisdom of the Colonial Office, and its profound knowledge of the Colonies, when it selected for a post of so much importance an Austrian for a colony almost entirely French, a man who had thrown over his religion for a Roman Catholic community, and an ex-lieutenant of the Austrian army in the very year when the French were driving the Austrians out of Italy! At the same time he was distinctly a clever man, full of vast projects, not one of which could he carry out; and incapable of treating his staff save as a sergeant treats the private soldier.

When I landed, there were exactly eleven paying students in the college; the rector had detached all the rest. I found the papers screaming against him everyday, I found the whole of the French population in open hostility, and I found the staff of the college in a spirit of sullen obstruction. We got along, however, somehow. More men came out from England, and, despite the chief, we managed to put things in some order. The pupils began to come back again; scholarships of £200 a year, tenable for four years in England, attracted them, and perhaps the new staff was more approved than the old. But the rector continued to quarrel with everybody. For a long time I succeeded in getting things carried on with some semblance of English order; but amicable relations were gradually dropped, for he was always intensely jealous of my authority and my popularity. Yet he could not manage without me, though he suspected, quite without any foundation, that I was the instigator of many of the attacks upon him. At last he ventured to attack me openly. It was the final act, and it was suicidal. For I took the very strong step of addressing a letter to the Governor, in which I accused my chief of a great many things which there is no need to repeat. It meant, of course, that these things had to be proved, or that I should be turned out of the service.

The Governor appointed a commission, and the rector was suspended during its sitting. It lasted nearly a year; at the end of that time two of the three commissioners reported that the charges wanted clearer proof, and the third commissioner refused to sign this report. The rector returned, but his rule was really over. I, who had been acting in command during the sitting of the commission, now claimed a year's furlough, and got it. Observe that there was no question of charging me with insubordination for attacking my chief; the facts were too obviously proved, as everybody could read for himself. I came home for a year's leave. Six months later the Legislative Council flatly refused supplies so long as the rector remained at the college. He was therefore sent home, and had influence enough to get a pension. They offered the rectorship to me; but I had had enough of educational work, and I declined it. At the end of my furlough, I stepped out into the world, without a pension, to begin all over again.

So much of my official life. The continual struggle worried me all the time, but perhaps it kept me alive. The rector had at least the power of making his enemies "sit up." In a tropical country it must be confessed that it is a great thing to be kept on the alert.

The staff of the college was a mixed lot; it consisted nominally of four or five "professors" and a dozen "junior masters." Among the former was my friend Frederick Guthrie, late Professor of Physics in the Royal School of Mines and founder of the Physical Society of London, a Fellow of the Royal Society, and a man of infinite good qualities. He was my most intimate friend from our first meeting in 1861 to his death in 1887. It is difficult to speak of him in terms adequate. He was a humourist in an odd, indescribable way; he did strange things gravely; he was a delightful donkey in money matters; when he drew his salary—£50 a month—he prepaid his mess expenses, and then stuffed the rest into his pocket and gave it to whoever asked for it, or they took it. Hence he was popular with the broken down Englishmen of shady antecedents who hung about Port Louis. He never had any money; never saved any; always muddled it away. Like many such men, he was not satisfied with his scientific reputation; he wanted to be a poet. He published two volumes of poetry, both with the same result. He was also clever as a modeller, but he neglected this gift. He did some good work in the colony in connection with the chemistry of the sugar-cane; he maintained a steady attitude of resistance to the rector, who could do nothing with him; and he resigned his post and came away from Mauritius at the same time as myself.

Another professor was a learned Frenchman named Léon Doyen. He had amassed an immense pile of notes for a history of the colony, but he died, and I know not what became of them. He lent me once a Ms. book full of notes, taken by himself as a student in Paris, of the lectures of Ampère on the formation and history of the French language. I copied all these notes, and used them for reading old French, in which language he lent me all the books he had. Some years later a book was published in England which contained these notes almost *verbatim*. I have often wondered whether Doyen's Ms. book furnished the material.

The masters were a wonderful scratch lot. There were two or three mulattos; one or two Frenchmen down on their luck; and the rest were broken Englishmen. One man had been a digger in Victoria; two had been in the army; another, it was discovered, had "served time" at Cape Town—him the Colonial Secretary put on board a sugar ship and sent back to his native country. I have often wondered who this man was, and what was his history; he had good manners—too good to be genuine; he was a fine and audacious liar; he had a good name. Fifteen years later I saw his death in the paper; he was then living in chambers in Pall Mall East.

The secretary of the college was a French Creole. His grandfather, who was still living in 1862 or 1863, an old man nearly ninety, was the Marquis de la Roche du Rouzit, and had formerly been page to Marie Antoinette. I once found him out, and talked with him, but he was too old—his memory was gone. He lived in a cottage, beside a most lovely bay among hills and woods; his principal occupation was angling for *ecrevisses* in the stream, and fishing in the bay from a dug-out. Yes—he remembered Antoinette. What was she like to look at? She was the Queen; they cut off her head; it was an infamy. Very little historical information was to be obtained from the old man; but he was very venerable of aspect, and looked, what he had always been, a gentleman of the old school.

There was another ancient person in the colony. He was the serving brother of the Masonic Lodges—the outer guard. At our dinners after lodge I used to get the old man to sit beside me and to talk. He had been in the roar of La Vendée; drummer-boy to La Roche Jaquelin. He grew animated when he talked of the battles and his escapes, and his precious drum. His daughters lived in the Seychelles, and made lovely fans from a certain palm leaf, I think. I have one still; that is, my daughter has it. I suppose that the good old drummer—"Aha! M'sieu—

j'étais le tambour, de La Roche Jaquelin—Oui—oui, M'sieu', moi qui vous le dis—le tambour"—is dead long ago.

It was a strange, confused, picturesque kind of life that one led there. The younger partners of the mercantile houses lived over their offices; one or two of the bank officials lived in the banks; the officers were in the barracks, always ready to come out and dine with the civilians; the Anglican bishop formed a centre of quiet life which was, to tell the truth, useful as an example; some of the Roman Catholic priests were very good fellows. Of course we made the great mistake of not seeing more of the French creoles, many of whom were highly cultivated and pleasant people; but they did not like the English rule, and they made no secret of their dislike. *Nous sommes un pays conquis* was the echo of their paper about once a week. And there were the planters.

There was one mercantile house where I was a frequent visitor. Two of the partners, both quite young men, ran a mess over their offices; there I met many of the skippers of the ships which brought out cargo to this firm. Sea-captains are an honest, frank and confiding folk. They have no suspicion or jealousies of their brother man, they have no private axe to grind, and they have a good many things to talk about. It was pleasant to call upon one on board his own ship and have him all to oneself in his cabin. One of them was a poet, he read me yards of his own poetry; another confided to me the miseries he endured at being separated from his wife; another told me yarns of things that he had witnessed—things *tacenda*. One, I remember, commanded a fine four-masted clipper which put in for repairs. She was bound for Trinidad with a cargo of Chinese coolies. The quarter deck was defended by four small cannonades loaded with grape; the captain's cabin had a fine stand of arms; every sailor carried a weapon of some kind; every officer had a revolver and could use it—and, mind, it takes a great deal of practice to use a revolver. They admitted up the hatchways about twenty coolies at a time and only for a few minutes; then they were driven below and another twenty came up; and so on all day. The captain told me that the coolies had knives; that there were women among them, for whom they fought; that the women were sick of it, and had mostly got through the port-holes and so drowned themselves; and that he was most anxious to get his repairs done and be off again, because every night some of the coolies got out and tried to swim ashore—which, he said, was a dead loss to everybody, including themselves, because the sharks got them all. In the little saloon of this ship was sitting a young Chinese lady, apparently all alone, but I suppose she had someone to look after her; she was beautifully dressed in thick silk, gleaming with gold thread.

Another man told me how, being then a mate, cholera broke out on board a ship bringing coolies from Calicut to Mauritius. All the patients either died or got well except one man. Now, if no one was down with cholera, the captain and the Indian apothecary, who served for doctor, could pretend that there was no sickness, and so get a clean bill of health. But if there was a single case on board, or anything to show that there had been an outbreak of cholera, they would have to go to Quarantine Island and there stay for six weeks after the last case. So, to make everything snug, they chucked the last patient overboard. After all, they did not get a clean bill, because the skipper and the apothecary quarrelled, and the latter split. Such were the tales they told.

Among my friends were two planters, whose hospitality to me was unbounded. The first was a gentleman—I use the word in its old and narrow sense—an Oxford man, a man of the finest manners, full of dignity and courtesy, a patriarch in his house. He used to invite me every year to spend Christmas with the party he got together. This party consisted of himself and madame, his three daughters, and his two sons. The bachelors all slept in a pavilion apart from the main house, where we had mattresses laid on the floor. Early in the morning, about half-past five, we were awakened, and after a cup of tea had a ramble in the woods and a bathe in the ravine. After breakfast, in the heat of the day, protected by big pith helmets, we went fishing in the stream. We fished for a large and very toothsome river fish called the *gourami*, and *gourami à la béchamel* is one of the finest preparations of fish that can be set before the most accomplished and finished *gourmet*. And the way of fishing was this. The river ran over and under boulders, at intervals opening into a small deep pool. We had a net and we all went into the water, swimming and pushing the net before us. When we got to the end of the pool one man dived down and pulled the fish out of the meshes of the net. We got back in the afternoon, and some of us slept off the fatigues and the heat of the morning. When the sun got low we walked about the lawns and among the flowers. At seven or so we sat down to dinner, and at ten we were all in bed.

The other planter was a Scotchman. I am ashamed when I think of the way I abused his hospitality; but it was his own fault, he always made me welcome and more than welcome. His estate—he belonged to the Clan Macpherson, and therefore the estate was called Cluny—lay on the other side of the island, not the Port Louis side. It was high up—about 1,600 feet above the sea level; it was always cool at night, and was carved out of the silent forest which lay all round it and shut it in. The place was most secluded and retired. The house was large and rambling, all on one floor, with half-a-dozen bedrooms, a dining-room, a salon, and a broad verandah. In the garden there were peach-trees—but the peaches would never ripen, strawberries—kept in the shade, green peas, celery, bananas, guavas—in short, all kinds of fruit, vegetables, and flowers. There was also a swimming-bath. In the morning I went out with the planter or his nephew, Mackintosh, on his daily visit to the fields. If we passed beyond the estate into the forest we came upon ravines, waterfalls, hanging woods, chattering monkeys, and deer in herds. The deer knew very well when it was close time; they would let you get near enough to see them clearly, then with a sudden alarm they would bound away, the graceful creatures. Two or three times I went shooting the deer; I am really grateful that I never got a shot at one, although I should certainly never have hit one had he been only a dozen yards away, because in all kinds of sport I have always been the worst of duffers. How can one be a good shot with eyes which are not only short-sighted but also slow-sighted?

There was a range of hills, on one side of which part of the estate lay. Macpherson planted the hill-side with coffee; but then came the heavy rains and washed his plants away, and there was an end of coffee planting on the island. Macpherson was too enterprising, however, and there were too many hurricanes, so he had to give up his estate. Mackintosh, his nephew, was put into another estate by one of the banks, and did well for a time; then his luck failed him, and he, too, had to resign. He was an asthmatic, and died at the age of five-and-thirty or so.

The most remarkable of the men I met in the island was my old friend James Longridge. He was the constructor of the railway; a Cambridge man, formerly articled to George Stephenson, a good mathematician, and a man full of inventions. His principal invention was the wire gun. A model of this gun he had mounted beside a quiet bay, where no one ever went, and he would make up small parties to experiment with it, firing across the bay. He offered the gun to the English Government; they kept him hanging on and off for some twenty years; at last, when he was past seventy years of age, they accepted it and gave him, in mockery, a pension of £200 a year—a pension at the age of seventy in return for a new gun, light, easily handled, and capable of any amount of development! I do not think that they have even called it the Longridge gun.

I have mentioned Quarantine Island. This was an island about thirty miles from Mauritius, in the Indian Ocean. It was provided with a lighthouse, and a medical man was always stationed there. If a ship put in with fever or cholera on board, she had to go to Quarantine Island, land her passengers, and wait there for the disease to work itself out. On one occasion a coolie ship was taken there with a frightful outbreak of cholera on board. Then one of the English doctors in Mauritius did a fine thing, for he volunteered to go and help the quarantine officer. Some hundreds died during this outbreak, but a great many were saved by the self-devotion of this man.

I knew the quarantine officer, who had been an army doctor. He once asked me to spend a fortnight with him. I accepted, taking the risk of a cholera ship being brought there, in which case I should have had to stay there and see it out. None came, however. It was a most curious experience. The island is about a mile and a half in circumference, surrounded by a kind of natural sea wall; a coral bank runs out all round except in two places. The doctor had a very good house all to himself. There were two men in charge of the lighthouse, there were a few Indian servants, and no one else was on the island except the ghosts of the dead who lie all over it. At sunset the Indians hastened to take refuge in their cottages; if they looked out after dark they saw white things moving about; there was no kind of doubt in their minds that they actually did see white things. I myself looked for them but saw nothing. How my friend could exist in such a solitude, with the unseen presence of the white things, was most amazing; it was, however, a great joy to him if he could catch a visitor. It was a very quiet fortnight. One day was exactly like another. We got up at six, before sunrise; we walked round the island twice, on the sea wall; we then bathed, but leisurely; bathing was only possible in very shallow water on account of "things." There was an astonishing quantity of "things" directly the water got a bit deeper. One had to keep on shoes on account of the *laff*, a small fish which lurks about the rocks with a poisonous backbone, which he sticks into the bather's foot and lames him for six months. There was also the *tazar*, a kind of sea-pike, which delights in biting a large piece out of a man's leg if he can get at him; there are young sharks; there are also the great sea slugs—the *bêche de mer*, which are not nice to step upon.

In one place, where the coral reef stopped, there was a curious pillar of rock about forty feet above the water and twenty or thirty feet in diameter. It stood a few yards from the shore, and was covered with innumerable wild birds. My friend would never shoot them; we would sit down by the shore and watch this multitude flying, screaming, fishing, fighting all day long. I know nothing about birds and have not the least idea of the names of these specimens; but of their numbers I have a lively recollection. In the transparent water between the shore and the rock there were water-snakes. I have never seen anything more beautiful than the motions of these creatures, darting about in all directions; they were of many colours and mostly, as it seems to my memory, about three feet long.

After getting through our exercise and our bathing we went through a form of dressing without putting on too much, and were ready for breakfast. There was always fish caught that morning, always curried chicken with claret, always coffee afterwards. Those days—alas! How good it was to be six-and-twenty! and what a perpetual feast was always present at breakfast and dinner!

Then came the cigar—it was before the days of the cigarette. Then a little game of *écarté* for six-pences; then a little reading; then in the heat of the day a *siesta*; at five o'clock we had tea; then, the heat of the day over, we once more marched round this island, looked at the birds and the snakes, bathed on the coral reef and at sunset sat down to dinner, which was just like breakfast—but perhaps more so. After dinner my host would touch the guitar, which he did very pleasantly; there would be another game of *écarté*, a little more tobacco, a brandy and soda, and so to the friendly shelter of the mosquito curtains. The lonely life among the dead men and their ghosts; the sea outside—a sea without a boat or a ship or a sail ever within sight, a sea filled with creatures; the silence broken only by the screaming of the sea-birds and the lapping of the waves, made up a strange experience, one to be remembered.

To return to the college staff; there was on it a man of curious antecedents and somewhat singular personality. To begin with, he never concerned himself in the least about money. He was a Scot of Aberdeen University; a scholar in his own way, which was not the way of Cambridge; a man of large reading in one Book. He was at this time—the sixties—about forty years of age. He never told me of his beginnings, which were, however, as I gathered from his knowledge of the shifts by which the poorer undergraduates of Aberdeen contrived to live, of a humble character. His first important post was that of missionary for some Scotch society to Constantinople, or Asia Minor—somewhere among the Turks. This post he held for a few years, during which he travelled about among the islands and had a very good time. He made no converts, but he argued from the Book with any who would listen to him, either among Greeks or Mohammedans. Then two things happened unto him: first, his conscience smote him, for drawing pay and writing reports about promising cases, days of enlargement, and signs of encouragement; second, he found that he no longer believed in the letter of his creed or in the letter of the Book. Therefore he resigned his post and set forth on his travels about the world armed with his Book and nothing else. A Scotchman finds friends in every colony. This man had no fear; he cast himself upon a place, stayed there till he was tired, and then went on somewhere else. He always had the Book in his hand; he was principally engaged, as he himself said, "among the minor prophets." I wish I could remember all the things he told me, but I know that according to his own account he was always making discoveries to the prejudice of Verbal Inspiration. "Obsairve" he said to me once, "Micah"—or was it Habakkuk?—"begins by saying 'The Lord spoke to me saying' . . . Now look here; later on he says, 'And then I knew that it was the Lord who spake to me.' So that the first words were only a formula." He grew tired of the place and shifted on. When I last heard of him he was running a school in some town near Melbourne. If he is still living, he must be eighty years of age. Heaven knows what discoveries he has made among the minor prophets.

Another member of the staff was a tall, thin German. He wore spectacles, he was horribly shy and nervous, spoke to no one, and lived all by himself in a little pavilion which was bedroom and keeping-room in one, for an Indian cook and all his goods. It was no use making overtures to him, for there was no response. He died of fever in 1867, and then I learned his history. He too had been a missionary; his field had been India; and like the Scotchman, he had found it impossible to pretend that he believed his creed; he too had given it up. He was in English holy orders, and his great dread was that the bishop would find him out and learn his history.

I wonder how many such missionaries there are. Once in Berlin I met a man of great learning and intelligence who gave me a similar experience. He had been in China for an American missionary society of the strictest creed. He was sent into the interior, where he mastered Chinese literature and grew to understand—as I think—the Chinese character. He told strange tales of tribes and peoples—China is a country of which we know nothing. Among others he found a tribe of Jews who had preserved nothing, not even the sacred books of their religion, except one kosher rite with reference to food. He made no converts, and by his narrow creed all these millions were doomed to everlasting torments. Heavens! what a creed! Everlasting torment for these ignorant folk, these women, these children! Are we monsters of cruelty that we should believe such things? Living by himself among them he gradually cast away the dreadful horrors of his sect and ceased to believe in the creed which he was paid to preach. So he too came out of it.

For a young man nowadays to reach the age of five-and-twenty or so, and to pass through the university, without coming across that common variety of man, the agnostic, would be impossible. Agnostics were much rarer forty or more years ago, but I made the acquaintance of two or three. One of them was an agnostic pure and simple, who thought it was his duty to learn such of the secrets of Nature as he could, and not to trouble himself about speculations as to the secrets of life, either before the cradle or after the grave—this was my friend Guthrie. Another was a more aggressive infidel, D. H——, a Prussian, a tall, handsome young man, then about thirty years of age. He had been in the Russian Army Medical Service, and was in Sebastopol during the siege. I wish I had written down all the things he told me about that siege, and the infernal rain of shells that fell upon the place night and day, with the hospitals crammed, not only with the wounded, but with men by hundreds stricken with cholera. However, when one is young one listens and forgets to take note of things. He was, as I have said, an aggressive infidel. Guthrie only said that it was not his business to inquire into things called spiritual, and he went so far as to deny the power of the Padre to learn more about these things than anyone else. D. H—— went much farther; he denied the whole of religion, the miraculous history, the inspiration, the doctrine, everything. He denied without bitterness, without contempt, without pity, without hatred; he simply denied and went his own way. He was as scientific a physician as one would find in the sixties. About the year 1866 he went away, and I learned presently that he had gone to Buenos Ayres, and that he had died of yellow fever, working in the hospitals there.

There was yet another kindly unbeliever of my acquaintance; he was a medical man and a botanist, and in both capacities he had accompanied a certain High Church mission to Central Africa, being one of the few survivors of an unlucky enterprise. He brought away with him a fever which never left him, and caused insomnia; he would sometimes lie sleepless for a week together, suffering prolonged tortures. In the intervals he sat up and poured out stories about his friends the missionaries; he loved them, and he laughed at them. He went with Bishop Ryan to Madagascar, and brought back more stories, which I hope the good bishop never heard. He was sent on a mission to look into the sugar-cane culture in various places, and died at Rangoon. I have never met his equal for humour; he bubbled over with humour; everything had its humorous side, and in his speech, or in his heart, there was never the slightest bitterness, or gall, or envy, or malice.

Religion sat very lightly upon the good folks of the colony. The French and the mulattos went to church—they had a cathedral, and a good many churches. The English had their cathedral, but they made very little use of it; they had also two or three little churches in the country, but they were not much frequented. The Scotch, for their part, waking one day to the understanding that they had no church, built one, and imported a clergyman. On the first day of service they all attended, on the following Sunday there was no one; and there has never been anyone since, except a few skippers and people of the port. There were also half-a-dozen missionaries. One of them founded a home for leprous children. Another rode about on a pony among the plantations, and said a word in season before dinner in the camps of the coolies—it was pleasant to read his report of "journeyings," and encouraging cases, and inquiries. The good man was not in the least a humbug; he only continued a perfunctory task, calling himself the sower of seed, long after the early enthusiasm of the outset had been chilled and destroyed. Another missionary of whom I have the liveliest recollection did gather round him a school of children, and a whole village, chiefly of negroes. He was a Swiss by birth, a cheery, hearty old man, very deaf, who talked in the simplest fashion to his flock. "Mes enfans," he would say, "qu'y en a qui fit créé le monde? Le Père Éternel—Qu'y en a qui fit sauvé le monde? Son fils, mes enfans— son fils. Et comment ce qui fait? C'est moi qui va vous le dire," and so on, in creole patois, while the shiny-faced blacks sat round him with open mouths. They never grew tired of hearing the old story, nor he of telling it. He made the Roman Catholics extremely jealous of his influence, especially over the children. Once one of their priests tried to draw the children away from his school. The pastor—he was a veritable pastor—sent him word that he would make a big gunny-bag and put him in it if he interfered. The Roman Catholic bishop, therefore, went to the Governor and laid a formal complaint and protest. "Did he really," asked the Governor, "threaten to put Father X—— in a gunny-bag?" "He did, indeed." "Then, my Lord Bishop," said the Governor, "I assure you that he is a man of his word; and *he'll do it*; he will indeed." Once I met him on the road, and inquired after his wife, who had been ill. I have said he was very deaf. He nodded his head several times, and shook me warmly by the hand. "My dear sir," he said, "I am always glad of a little conversation with you. That is precisely the view concerning Moses and geology which I have always taken."

I must get on with my gallery of colonials. Among them were the late Sir Edward Newton, afterwards Colonial Secretary of Jamaica; Sir William Marsh, Colonial Secretary of Hong Kong, Auditor-General of Cyprus, and Acting Governor of Hong Kong; Sir John Douglas, afterwards Lieutenant-Governor of Ceylon. The Governors in my time were Sir William Stevenson, who died there, and Sir Henry Barkly, who lived to a great age and died only the other day. Dr. Ryan was the Anglican Bishop, a good scholar, a man of many gifts, but somewhat narrow in his views. The Chief Justice was a Scotchman named Shand; I believe that he was a good lawyer and a good judge. He was a cousin of one of the Scottish judges—Lord Shand. The Puisne judges were for the most part, if I remember aright, creoles of the island. The master of the Supreme Court was a man who had the reputation of a good lawyer, and was also a *gourmet*. It was a great thing to dine with him, because he used to stay at home all day in anxious consultation with the cook; it was informing to sit next to him at a public dinner, because he would discourse learnedly on the great art and science of dining. He once told me a little story about his own skill. "I was with a fishing party," he said, "in Scotland, being then a young man. I met with a slight accident and sprained my ankle. 'Go without me,' I told my friends. 'This evening you shall have a surprise.'" He stopped with a sigh. "Twenty years after," he continued, "I was in Westminster Hall when a man accosted me. 'Mr.——,' he said. 'That, sir,' I told him, 'is my name, but for the moment I do not recollect yours.' 'Never mind the name,' he said. 'Eh! man! That surprise! That saumon soup!'"

We had among us a great light in meteorology—the place was a most important meteorological station—named Charles Meldrum; he was made a Fellow of the Royal Society, to his infinite gratification. There was a merchant, also, whom I remember. He was already an old man in the sixties. His distinctive point was that he was a friend of Carlyle, and I heard the other day that he was dead at a very great age, having gone to Ecclefechan to spend his last days. There was a charming and delightful bank manager named Anderson, who in London as a young man had been one of an interesting circle of Bohemians—the later Bohemians. The circle is described in a novel or a series of chapters, called *Friends of Bohemia*, by one of them, Edward M. Whitty. Anderson was a man of great culture; an early worshipper of Browning, Holman Hunt, and Burne Jones. He himself once produced a small volume of Browning-esque verse, but somehow did not like to be reminded of it. He came home and was made a Director of the Oriental Bank. He was also a member of the Savile Club, where I met him later.

One more figure, this time one better known to fame. Among the younger merchants was a man named Dykes Campbell. He was one of those who have literary proclivities without any particular gifts of imagination or expression. Most men of this kind try the impossible and produce bad verse and bad fiction. Campbell did nothing of the kind; he kept up his reading, he went on with his work, and at the age of forty or so he found he could retire with a competence. Then he came to England and devoted himself for ten years to the investigation of everything relating to Coleridge; and he ended by producing the best life of Coleridge that we have, and the best, I suppose, that we shall ever have. So this simple colonial merchant has made an enduring mark in the literature of the century. It is really a remarkable story. Campbell did nothing else worth mentioning. He wrote a little towards the end of his life for the *Athenæum*, but he formed no other project of serious work, and he died at the age of fifty-five.

On the intellectual side of the colony one need not linger long; nor need we press the matter too hardly. For without stimulus, without papers and journals, without new books, and without learned bodies, how can there be any intellectual life? The newspapers of the colony were contemptible; there was a so-called "Royal Society," which had a museum and a curator, but there was no life in it; there was a Meteorological Society, which had a committee, and a secretary, Meldrum, but the secretary alone did all the work, which was, as I have said, of great importance. There were no lectures, partly because no one would go out in the evening except to dinner, while no one would go to a lecture before dinner, and partly because everybody knew everybody else, and could get any information that he might want without the trouble of going to a lecture. A few private persons had small collections of books, but there was not much reading. There was a circulating library, which was very poorly supported; there was a subscription library, which fell to pieces, and what became of the books I could never learn. The college had a library containing a very fine collection of historical works.

For my own part, as a full quarter of the year was vacation, I naturally fell back upon work. In fact I did a great deal of work of a desultory kind. I filled up many important gaps. The most important part of my reading was in French. My friend Léon Doyen introduced me to the study of old French, and gave me the key; he also lent me certain books of old French. Then I found a man who had a complete edition of Balzac, and another who had a complete edition of Georges Sand. I worked through all these books. And I found another man with a collection of old numbers of the *Revue des Deux Mondes*. I do not think that any English magazine contains so many articles of enduring interest as this review. And I was writing all the time. I wrote essays for the most part, which have long since been torn up. In truth I was not in the least precocious, and I spent these years in getting control over my pen, which at first ran along of its own accord, discursive, rambling, and losing its original purpose. No one would believe the trouble I had in making the pen a servant instead of a master; in other words, in forcing the brain to concentration. I had by this time quite abandoned higher mathematics, which from this point of view was a loss, because there is nothing that fixes and concentrates the attention more than mathematics. I found, however, that the writing of verse was useful in the same direction, and I wrote a good deal of verse, none of which have I ever ventured to publish.

I also wrote a novel. It was a long novel, intended for the then orthodox three volumes. I wrote it with great enjoyment, and I persuaded myself that it was good. Finally I sent it to England and had it submitted to a publisher. His verdict was in plain language—"Won't do; but has promise." When I got home I received back the MS., and I agreed with the verdict; it was a happy thing for me that the MS. was not published. The papers lay in my chambers for a long time afterwards in a corner covered with dust. They got upon my nerves. I used to see a goblin sitting on the pile; an amorphous goblin, with tearful eyes, big head, shapeless body, long arms and short legs. He would wag his head mournfully. "Don't make another like me," he said. "Not like me. I couldn't bear to meet another like me." At last I plucked up courage and burned the whole pile. Then my goblin vanished and I saw him no more. I expected him sometime after, if only to thank me for not making another like him. But he came not, and I have often wondered whither that goblin went for rest and consolation.

It was, I think, in 1864 that I became aware of an increased tendency to a form of melancholia which made me uneasy at first. Gradually the symptom became a burden to me. I suppose it was caused partly by over-work; partly by worry on account of my exasperating chief; and partly by the monotony of a climate which was sometimes much too hot, and sometimes a little too wet, but never cold. Some men are so constituted that they enjoy this eternal summer; some cannot stand it. I was one of the latter class. As the thing grew worse, I took advice of my German friend. He advised an immediate change of scenery, if not of climate. Accordingly I took the first opportunity of a vacation to visit the Island of Réunion, formerly called Bourbon. I recorded my impressions of the place in *Once a Week* (see *Once a Week*, Oct. 16th and Oct. 23rd, 1869), a circumstance to which I shall refer again.

My residence in Mauritius of six years was full of experiences. In 1862 we had an attack of cholera, not, happily, very severe nor of long duration. It carried off, however a good many whites. It was the second attack that had visited the island, that of 1854, its predecessor, being far more virulent and lasting much longer. There was a hurricane one year, which wasted the whole island and destroyed an immense quantity of canes—but how sweet and pure was the air of the place after it! On another occasion a waterspout burst in the hills round the town, and floods of water five or six feet deep rushed through the streets, tearing up the cottages of wattle-and-daub, washing the town, and drowning more people than were ever counted.

The last experience was that of a city in a plague. In 1866–67 broke out for the first time the Mauritius fever. Up to that time the place was considered as healthy as any island or country in the temperate zone. There were no endemic disorders, and everybody lived to a green old age. Now my friend D. H——, when he went away in 1865, gave utterance to a medical prophecy. He said, "You have 250,000 coolies on this little island, without counting negroes, Malagasy men, Malays, and Chinese. None of them will obey any sanitary rules; the soil of the town, and even that of the cane-fields, is saturated. Sooner or later, there will be a great outbreak of fever or plague."

This prophecy was fulfilled to the letter. The fever appeared; it ran through the Indian camps and the negro villages with frightful rapidity; it attacked white as well as coloured people in certain districts, especially low-lying or swampy places. It was not sporadic; it caught whole families and carried them off. For instance, the railway people wanted a party of coolies to be taken from one place to another. The sirdar who was entrusted with the business brought them, with their wives and children, to the town and lodged them in an old room formerly used for slaves. This done, he was taken with the fever and died. Then all the coolies were taken with it; no one knew they were in Port Louis, no doctor went near them, and they all died where they lay. All the quinine in the place was exhausted; that which had been ordered from Europe was by mistake sent out round the Cape instead of by the overland route; what there was sold for £30, and more, an ounce.

The number of deaths rose to three hundred a day for the whole island; in Port Louis alone to one hundred and more; the shops were closed; the streets were silent; the funerals went on all day long in the Roman Catholic churches, and in their cemetery the priests stood over open *fosses communes*, saying the last prayers for the dead without intermission as the coffins were brought in and laid side by side.

My residence was then about ten miles from town, on a plateau 1200 feet above the level of the sea. We had some fever, but not much; our servants' camp contained a few patients, and we doctored them ourselves with good results. It was a strange experience. There were dreadful stories of suffering. The Chinese who had escaped the cholera were laid low with the fever, and of the mulattos no one knew who had died or how many. When the canes were cut, dead bodies were found among them of poor wretches who had crept in to die at peace under these waving plumes of grey. When all was over it was found that the savings bank had $30,000 lying in its hands which were never claimed;

the investors with all their families had been wiped out. The worst was just over when I went away in June 1867. But fever still lingered, and is now endemic as one of the conditions of life in the colony as much as it is in Sierra Leone and on the West Coast of Africa.*

---

* A Fever Inquiry Commission was appointed by Sir Henry Barkly in 1867, and a sub-committee reported to this commission in 1868 upon the epidemic. The sub-committee decided that the epidemic was one of malarious fever, showing itself under various forms, and pointed out that on December 31st, 1866, when the epidemic was approaching, the number of immigrants from India alone had reached the enormous figure of 246,049. The report confirms Sir Walter Besant's recollections. Estimating the population of Port Louis at 80,000 in 1867, it shows that the death-rate during the year amounted to 274 per thousand. The greatest mortality in one day, April 27th, was 234. It was established that many hundreds of lives were lost during the epidemic through the want of cleanliness and overcrowding in the Indian and creole camps.

VIII

ENGLAND AGAIN: THE PALESTINE
EXPLORATION FUND

With a year's furlough on half-pay, I bade farewell to my friends. I was in no hurry to get home, and therefore took a passage by the Cape steamer. We were connected with Cape Town by a service of two or three little steamers. One of them had just gone down in a storm while lying in harbour at the Cape, a fact which, had I known it, would probably have sent me home by the shorter and safer route. But it was a chance which might never offer itself again of seeing the Cape.

So we started in our cockle-shell. There was no place for stores of dead stock, no ice-rooms or anything of that sort; we had our sheep and our poultry stowed away in pens somewhere in the bows. We started with very fine weather, though in mid-winter, for South Africa; we put in at Durban, but not to land; we skirted along the coast then called No Man's Land, where we saw the Caffres walking about; and we landed at Port Elizabeth, where we had time to look round. A man who could talk Caffre carried me off to show me a kraal. We found Port Elizabeth provided with fine stone warehouses, waiting for the trade of the future.

That evening it began to blow. Off the Cape of Good Hope— formerly the Cape of Torments—the wind is believed to blow harder and the sea to rise higher than in any other part of the globe. We proved that this belief is well founded. The night was unendurable in the cabin; two of us spent it in the small smoking-saloon for'ard, wrapped in a plaid. In the middle of the night a huge sea broke over the ship, smashed in the doors of the saloon and carried them out to sea; very luckily it did not carry us out to sea with the doors. When the day broke at last we found that all our live stock—our sheep and fowls, with their pens—had been carried away. The waves were mountainous. Presently there was a great shouting and whistling; the sea had torn up the engine room hatchway, and put out four of the five fires; a tarpaulin was rigged on hastily; but we had but one fire left for a time.

All that day, with the other man, my companion of the smoking-saloon, we clung to the davits watching the waves. Everytime we rose to the top of a wave, our hearts sank at looking into the surging valley below; when we were down, the mountain before us seemed as if it must swamp and sink us. This lasted for four days and four nights. It was a brave and a staunch little ship, and when the gale at last abated it was found that we had been driven two hundred and fifty miles south of our course. Since we had come out of the storm in safety, it was a small thing that we had nothing but pork in various forms to live upon until we got to Cape Town. The delay caused us to lose our steamer for Southampton. I, for one, however, was quite content to stay a fortnight at Cape Town and to look around.

I suppose the place is altered in thirty years. In 1867 it was a sleepy, pleasant, sunshiny town, with lovely gardens. There was a college, and there was a House of Commons, and there were the vineyards and the wine-making to see. There were plenty of people at the hotel. I called upon Mr. Southey, the Minister; he showed me the first diamond ever found in South Africa, a thing as big as the top of a child's little finger. I attended a debate at the House, and was pleased to observe Mr. Southey's patience with the farmers who were the members. First, he stated his case, quite clearly; then the members rose one after the other and stated that they understood nothing; Mr. Southey stated it again, in other words, quite patiently; again they got up and betrayed profound misunderstanding; a third time he put the case, always with patience and without temper, and then they began to understand.

In the evening there was always a gathering of the members at the hotel. Those who had come from England talked about the old country with affection. One of them, an old gentleman of eighty-four, who afterwards danced a hornpipe to show his agility, said that he came from Fetter Lane. I asked him if he had ever met Charles Lamb. He had not, he said, but he knew Samuel Lamb the butcher. The Afrikander Bond in these days had not been invented, and if the Dutch had begun to dream of sweeping the English into the sea, they had kept their dreams to themselves, so far as I know. It was winter, but the sun was pleasant, and the air was warm, and I left after my brief stay with real regret. We had a delightful voyage, with no bad weather at either end. We saw Ascension and landed at St. Helena, having time to drive up to Longwood and see Napoleon's last residence. I should say that there are worse places to live in than St. Helena; it is full of flowers and the trade breeze is always cool.

And so, after six years and a half, I landed again at Southampton. The time had completely changed the whole current of my thoughts—

my views of society, order, religion, everything. I went out with my head full of university and ecclesiastical prejudices. I believe that I lost them all. Gentle reader, a man who has had six years of life in a colony such as Mauritius, where all kinds of men are always coming and going, where one meets men of every station and every country, where life is carried on under conditions which cannot exist in England, may become anything you please—but if he takes to literature, he can never become a prig; nor, if he takes to politics, can he ever become the advocate of a ruling caste; nor can he pursue the old narrow views of ecclesiastical religion. He becomes more human; he has learned at least the lesson that in humanity there is no caste that is common, and none that is unclean. The unclean and the common are individual, and not general. It is a simple lesson, but it was—oh!—so very much wanted in the sixties.

Another thing that I found, and remember, is that in the colonies there are so many good fellows. There is less struggle, less posing, less intriguing, less serving of personal interest than we find at home; less envy, less jealousy, less malice; more friendliness, more hospitality, more kindliness; and less caste. Let me be always thankful for my colonial experience.

I began life again at the age of thirty-one. My capital was a pretty extensive knowledge acquired by voracious and indiscriminate reading. I could write, I knew, pretty well, having got over that difficulty of which I have spoken. I had a special branch of knowledge, in which I was not likely at that time to find many rivals, though since then the enormous increase of writers has caused an increase of competitors in every branch, including old French literature. What would happen I knew not, but of these things I was resolved—I would not go back to the Royal College of Mauritius, nor would I undertake a mastership in any English school. I was never a teacher to the manner born, nor did I ever take really kindly to the work. As regards ways and means, I had a whole twelvemonth on half-pay to look about me, and I had a few—a very few—hundreds in my pocket.

A man who goes away at four-and-twenty and comes back at one-and-thirty speedily discovers that his old place among his friends is filled up. In seven years they have gone off on different roads, they have made new associates, the old ties are broken. Moreover, in whatever direction such a man after seven years' absence turns, he is met by the opposition and the competition of those younger than himself, who are backing up each other. Besides, it is felt that a man who goes out to a colony ought—I know not why—to remain there. Under similar circumstances, it would be now much more difficult for the returned colonial to make an opening than it was thirty years ago. I understood that my opening was to be made—somehow or other, as yet I knew not how—by literature. It was a resolution which one had to keep to oneself Everybody ridiculed it; an attempt to live by literature was considered certain dependence and beggary; indeed, there were examples in plenty to warrant that prejudice. Thirty years ago we were not far from the memory of literary Bohemia, which used to be freely painted in colours so rosy, yet was a country so full of privation, debt, duns, and dependence. I had no intention whatever of joining the Bohemians. I say that I did not quite know what I should do; but I was resolved that I would not become a publisher's hack; that I would not hang about publishers' offices and beg for work; nor write introductions and edit new editions at five guineas the job with a preface, an introductory life, notes, and an index thrown in. I meant to get on by means of literature and live an independent life. Understanding, as I do now, the difficulties which lay in the way before me, I am amazed when I consider the absolute confidence with which I regarded the future.

My furlough I spent in reading and in travelling about England, of which I had seen, hitherto, so very little. As regards serious work, I put together my papers, notes, and studies, and wrote a book on Early French Poetry, which was published in the autumn of 1868. The book did not profess to be a history; it was simply a collection of separate studies. It did as well as one could have expected from the nature of the subject; it introduced me to the world as a specialist who could discourse pleasantly on a subject hitherto treated, if at all in this country, by Dryasdust—I may be permitted to say so much in my own praise. There was an edition of 750 copies printed, of which a good many were satisfactorily disposed of. The arrangement was that which is humorously called "half profits," and my share was II*s*. 8*d*. or 8*s*. II*d*., or some such great sum. Of course I now understand what it meant; but the amount of profit in such a case mattered nothing—the advantage to me was enormous. If my publishers had made the condition that the II*s*. 8*d*. or the 8*s*. II*d*. should be their own, I should have accepted their terms joyfully for the sake of the introduction to the public.

In June 1868 a great piece of luck came to me in the shape of a post as secretary to a society. It was exactly what I wanted; the salary was sufficient for bread and cheese, the hours were not excessive, leaving plenty of time for my own work, and the associations were eminently respectable. It was the Society for the Systematic and Scientific Exploration of Palestine. Thomson, Archbishop of York, was our chairman; our general committee contained a most imposing list of names; and on our executive committee were James Glaisher, F.R.S., afterwards chairman; W.S.W. Vaux, the numismatist; Canon Tristram, F.R.S.; Hepworth Dixon, the editor of the *Athenæum*—he died at Christmas 1879; James Fergusson, F.R.S., the writer on architectural history; J.L. Donaldson, professor of architecture; William Longman, publisher; Professor Hayter Lewis, architect, and successor of Professor Donaldson; Walter Morrison, M.P.; Sir George Grove, afterwards Director of the College of Music; and the Rev. F.W. Holland, who spent most of his holidays in the peninsula of Sinai.

For eighteen years I continued to be the paid secretary of this society. During that time were conducted the excavations at Jerusalem by Captain (now Sir Charles) Warren; the survey of Western Palestine by Captain (now Colonel) Conder and Captain Kitchener (now Lord Kitchener); and the Geological Survey of Palestine by Professor Hull, F.R.S.—besides the Archæological Survey by M. Clermont Ganneau. The work of the society has, in fact, completely changed the whole of the old geography, topography, and archæology of the Holy Land; it has restored to the Temple its true grandeur, and to Jerusalem its ancient splendour; it has shown the country, formerly populous and highly cultivated, dotted over with strong and great cities—Tiberias alone, which had been called a little fishing village, has been proved to have been a city with a wall as great in extent as the wall of the City of London. The work brought me into personal contact with a great number of men eminent in many ways. Among them I may mention the philanthropic Lord Shaftesbury, Sir Moses Montefiore, Professor Pusey, A.J. Beresford-Hope, General Charles Gordon, Laurence Oliphant, Sir Charles Wilson, Sir Charles Warren, Lord Kitchener, and Sir Richard Burton, to say nothing of many bishops, scholars, and archæologists.

I remained, as I said, as paid secretary for about eighteen years, and as honorary secretary I have remained ever since. During my official work as paid secretary I made many friends by means of the society. First and foremost among them was Edward Palmer, Lord Almoner's Professor of Arabic in the University of Cambridge. That great linguist and fine

Oriental scholar explored for the society, with the late W.T. Tyrwhitt Drake, the Desert of the Wanderings. He could enter into and understand every man's brain; he had that quick sympathy, that feminine perception of things, which make the thought-reader. No man that I ever met with in this my earthly pilgrimage has been able so profoundly to impress his personality upon his friends. He was a great scholar, yet had none of the scholarly dignity; he mostly sat telling stories and bubbling over with natural mirth. He was always doing strange and unexpected things. Once the whole town was placarded with posters, half in English, half in Arabic; again, Palmer invented a new and surprising trick which was brought out at the old Polytechnic; on another occasion he presented his friends with a volume of serious poetry; then with a burlesque; then he translated the Koran, dictating it in a sort of monotone, as if he were reading the original in a mosque. In appearance he was a remarkable being: a little man with a large head, curiously delicate features, a hand like a woman's, eyes unnaturally bright, brown hair, and a long silky beard. When he was eighteen, being then in a City office, he was sent home to die of consumption; but he did not die; he diverted his thoughts from death by learning Arabic and Persian, but he always preserved the delicate complexion. He suffered from asthma, which hardly ever left him.

Till the age of thirty-eight or so he lived at Cambridge, lecturing, reading, teaching, examining, and picking up new languages everyday. Then a great change came upon his life. Through the failure of a cousin he became involved to the extent of some £1,500. He had not a penny; moreover, his wife was living in France—or rather dying in France—which obliged him to keep up a separate establishment and to be running over to Paris continually to look after her. He made an arrangement with his creditors. He assigned to them his fellowship and professorship—about £400 a year—until they should be paid in full, and he came to London penniless, but full of confidence. He became a leader-writer for the *Standard*, and there was never any further trouble about money except that he always spent everything as fast as it came in. In 1882, when the trouble with Egypt began, and the Suez Canal was threatened, he undertook for the Government a journey in the Sinai Desert in order to keep the Arabs quiet. He went out alone; disguised as a Syrian Effendi, he travelled through the desert in the height of the summer heat; he saw sheikh after sheikh, and made them promise not to harm the canal; he arrived safely at Suez, his mission accomplished. He had, however, to take some money to his new allies, and was treacherously murdered by a party of Arabs sent from Cairo for the purpose. The murder, like everything else that belongs to Palmer's history, had in it all the elements of the picturesque, the weird, and the wonderful. The party were caught in the night, and all night long the captors discussed what should be done with their prisoners. They were afraid of murdering them for some reason; probably Palmer's guides filled them with terror, telling them how great a man was the Effendi Abdullah, what a power among the Sinai Arabs, what a scholar. But at last their obedience to their chiefs overcame terror. They ran upon Palmer with swords, and threw his bleeding body over the crags and rocks into the valley below. And so they treated his companions Gill and Charrington. Sir Charles Warren, sent out for the purpose, hunted down and hanged everyone of the murderers. Palmer's portrait hangs in the hall of St. John's College, Cambridge, but I fear that his history is no longer remembered by the undergraduates.

Let me give here a certain elegy which I wrote for the Rabelais Club of which Palmer was a member:—

THE DEATH OF THE SHEIKH ABDULLAH.

"*The blood-red dawn rolls westward; crag and steep*
Welcome the splendid day with purple glow;
Through the dim gorges shape and outline creep,
And deeper seem the black depths far below.

"*Earth hath no wilder place her lands among;*
Here is no cool green spot, no pleasant thing;
No shade of lordly bough, no sweet birds' song,
No gracious meadows, and no flowers of spring.

"*The eagle builds his eyrie on these peaks;*
Below the jackal and hyena prowl:
No gentle creature here her pasture seeks,
But fiery serpents lurk, and vulture foul.

"*I see a figure, where the rock sinks sheer*
Into a gorge too deep for noontide sun;
Above, the sky of morning pure and clear—
Others are there, but I see only one.

"In Syrian robes, like some old warrior free,
After fierce fight a captive, so he stands,
Gazing his last—sweet are the skies to see,
And sweet the sunshine breaking o'er the lands.

"Then, while the light of wrath prophetic fills
His awful eyes, he hurls among his foes—
Wild echoes ringing round the 'frighted hills—
A flaming prophecy of helpless woes.

"Yea; like a Hebrew Prophet doth he tell
Of swift revenge and death and women's moan;
And stricken babes and burning pains of hell.
Then each man's traitor heart fell cold as stone.

"And through their strong limbs fearful tremblings crept,
And brown cheeks paled, and down dropped every head;
Then, with a last fierce prophecy he leaped.
* * * * *
My God! Abdullah—Palmer—art thou dead?"

A society such as the Palestine Exploration Fund naturally attracts all the cranks, especially the religious cranks. There was one man who was a mixture of geographical science and of religious crankiness. He claimed to be the son of the founder of the Plymouth Brethren; he had vast ideas on the rebuilding of Babylon, that it might once more become the geographical centre of European and Asiatic trade. As a matter of fact we only have to consider the position of Babylon in order to understand that when the country is taken over by a European Power, and the valley of the Euphrates is once more drained and cultivated, that great city will again revive. But with this insight he mixed up a queer religion, in which Nimrod played a great part. He would talk about Nimrod as long as I allowed him. And then I heard of a grand project in which he was concerned. It was nothing less than the cutting of a sea-canal from the northern end of the Gulf of Akaba to the south of the Dead Sea; this canal would flood the Jordan valley and create a large central lake over that valley extending for some miles on either hand. Then, with a short railway across Galilee, there would be a new waterway, with possible extension by rail and canal to Persia and India.

The project was seriously considered; a meeting was held in the office of the Palestine Exploration Fund, at which the then Duke of Sutherland and others consulted Sir Charles Warren and Captain Conder on the possibility of constructing the canal. The duke could not, or would not, be persuaded that a cutting for so many miles of seven hundred feet deep at least would be practically impossible. I think there must have been some political business at the back of the project, of which, however, nothing more was heard.

The man who could read all ancient inscriptions by means of the original alphabet, entirely constructed of equilateral triangles, was amusing at first but became tedious. The man who saw "Nature Worship," to use the common euphemism, in everything ancient also became tedious. The man who wanted the society to send out an expedition to Ararat for the recovery of the Ark, was extremely interesting. The Ark, it seems, is lying embedded in ice and snow on the top of that mountain; all we have to do is to blow up the ice with dynamite, when the Ark will be revealed. The man who knew where to lay his hand upon the Ark of the Covenant, if we would send him out for the purpose, was perhaps a knave, perhaps a crank. But crankery and knavery sometimes overlap. The man who knew where the monks buried their treasure on the fall of the Latin Kingdom was also perhaps knave and perhaps crank. He had got hold of an Italian book about buried treasure in Palestine, and believed it.

Then there was a man who had a road upon his mind. It is a road in Eastern Palestine, which has milestones upon it, and is a well constructed road, and starts right into the desert. Where does it go? He was always inquiring about this road; and indeed it is a very curious thing that the road, mentioned by Gibbon, should have been so carefully constructed, and one would really like to know where it goes. The man who could prove that Mount Sinai is not Hor and that the survey of the Sinai peninsula was therefore a useless piece of work, wrote a book about it, and so relieved his mind. He was an interesting man; he had been an army surgeon in the Crimea; then he became a barrister, and got into notice by defending the prisoner charged with the Clerkenwell explosion; then he became a leader-writer for the *Morning Post*, with this fad about Mount Sinai to keep him in a wholesome condition of excitement and interest. I know not how many converts he made, but I think, for my own part, that he was perhaps right.

In the course of my work at the Palestine Exploration Society I was connected officially with one great discovery and one great fraud. The discovery was that of the Moabite Stone—an event which forced the world to acknowledge the historical character of part, at least, of the Old Testament. The discovery was made by a German missionary employed by an English society. Being in English employment, he communicated his discovery to the German Court. At the same time M. Clermont Ganneau, then *chancelier* of the French Consulate, heard of it, and Warren heard of it. Negotiations were briskly begun; but the Arabs, in the end, thinking that it was a magical stone, since so many Europeans wanted to get it, broke it to pieces. Then Warren procured squeezes of the inscription, which were sent home. These precious documents we had photographed. The treasurer of the society, Mr. Walter Morrison, kindly shared with me the task of watching the work in the photographer's studio, because we were afraid of letting the documents go out of our sight and our hands. When we had our photographs, the squeezes became less valuable. We sent copies round to the best known Hebrew scholars, and all began to write books and monographs. We found a great quantity of things in the course of our excavations and our surveys, but never again did we make so splendid a "find" as that of the Moabite Stone.

Some years later—I think about 1877—a certain Shapira, a Polish Jew converted to Christianity but not to good works, came to England and called upon me mysteriously. He had with him, he said, a document which would simply make students of the Bible and Hebrew scholars reconsider their ways; it would throw a flood of light upon the Pentateuch; and so on. The man was a good actor; he was a man of handsome presence, tall, with fair hair and blue eyes; not the least like the ordinary Polish Jew, and with an air of modest honesty which carried one away. What was his discovery? First he would not tell me. Then I said that he might go away. So he told me. It was nothing less than a contemporary copy of the book of Deuteronomy written on parchment. A contemporary copy! Could I see it? I might see a piece, which he pulled out of his pocket-book. It was written in fine black ink, as fresh after three thousand years as when it was laid on; and in the Phœnician characters of the Moabite Stone. It had been preserved, he told me, through being deposited in a perfectly dry cave in Moab. Then I suggested that he should make this discovery known to the world. He consented, after a while, to reveal it to two persons. Dr. Ginsburg, the great Hebrew scholar, and Captain Conder, the Surveyor of Western Palestine. I undertook to invite them to come on the morrow. But

Ginsburg considered that the invitation included his friends, and so the whole of the British Museum, so to speak, with all the Hebrew scholars in London, turned up, and with them Conder. Shapira unfolded his MS. amid such excitement as is very seldom exhibited by scholars. The exposition lasted about three hours; then Shapira tore off a piece of the precious document to show the nature of the parchment. It was, as one of the company remarked, wonderfully modern in appearance, and a remarkable illustration of the arts as known and practised in the time of Moses. Then Shapira withdrew; and after a little conversation the learned company separated. As they went out, one of them, a professor of Hebrew, exclaimed with conviction, "This is one of the few things which could not be a forgery and a fraud!"

There were left with me Captain Conder and William Simpson, of the *Illustrated London News*. Said Simpson dryly, "He values his MS. at a million. Of course he could spare the value of the bit he tore off. I suppose it is worth £500." So he chuckled and went his way. Simpson entertained a low view of the worthy Shapira, Christian convert. Then Conder, who had been very quiet, only putting in a little question from time to time, spoke. "I observe," he said, "that all the points objected to by German critics have vanished in this new and epoch-making *trouvaille*. The geography is not confused, and Moses does not record his own death."

"Well?" I asked, for more was in his face.

"And I know, I believe, all the caves of Moab, and they are all damp and earthy. There is not a dry cave in the country."

"Then you think——?"

"Precisely."

Clermont Ganneau, who was in Paris, came over to see the precious MS. A few days passed; the learned divines and professors were hanging over the MS. preparing their commentaries. Ganneau asked permission to see the MS., and then all the fat was in the fire. "I know," he said, "how this MS. was obtained. The parchment is cut from the margins of Hebrew manuscripts, some of them of considerable antiquity. The writing is that of yesterday."

Alas! that was so. That was exactly what had been done. Shapira received his MS. back without any offer of a hundred pounds, not to speak of a million. It was too much for the poor man; the work had cost him so much trouble, he had reckoned with so much faith on the success of his careful and learned forgery, that his mind became unhinged.

He hanged himself. I believe that the disappointment of the Hebrew scholars, who had begun learned books on the newly discovered text, was pitiful. Shapira left with me, and it was never reclaimed, the leaden cover of Samson's coffin. Yes, nothing less than the coffin of Samson Agonistes, Samson the strong, Samson the victim of woman's wiles. Shapira said that he was not absolutely certain about it; he should be most sorry to mislead; the truth was that he could not be sure; but there was on the leaden roll the name, nowhere else occurring in Hebrew literature: the actual name of Samson in Phœnician characters—plain for all to read.

There were many more days of discovery and murmured discovery; arrivals of drawings, copies of inscriptions, statuettes, and other things, all of which kept that quiet office alive. Conder discovered old towns and sites by fifties; Ganneau found the head of the Roman statue set up by the Romans on the site of the Holy of Holies; he also found the stone of the Temple warning strangers not to cross the barrier on pain of death. Gordon found, as he thought, the true place of the Crucifixion; and there was always running on the old controversy about the sacred site. For my part I have always agreed with Conder that when a site is accepted by tradition common to Christian, Jew, and Moslem, that site is probably correct; the excavations and discoveries made on the site of the traditional Holy Sepulchre continually furnished new arguments in favour of that tradition, and history seems to me to be entirely on that side.

As we wanted as much history as we could get, I created a small society among the people interested in these things for the translation and publication of the ancient pilgrimages. We had about one hundred and twenty members. One translation was done by Aubrey Stewart, late Fellow of Trinity College, Cambridge; Guy L'Estrange, Conder, and one or two more helped; Sir Charles Wilson annotated the books. In about ten years we accomplished the task that we had set before us in our original prospectus—we had translated the writings of all the old pilgrims. I am quite sure that no society ever before did so much with so small an income. To be sure, we had no office clerks to pay; and our work was mostly gratuitous. I have always been proud of my share in creating this subsidiary society and in producing this series. The work will certainly never be done again. There were so few copies—not more than two hundred, I believe—that our labours are practically unknown except to those who study the topography, the geography, and the buildings of the Holy Land.

WALTER BESANT

The work of the main society all this time was going on quietly. I had organised a system of local societies all over the country, and had sent lecturers to explain what we were doing. Consequently I was enabled to supply our party in Palestine with ample funds. The survey cost in round figures £200 a month; and when Clermont Ganneau went out for us on a special archæological mission, he wanted about £100 a month more. The public interest in our proceedings was maintained by the publication of the society's quarterly journal. There were, however, naturally times of doubt and trouble. Thus, in 1874—when I had to find all the money month by month, to translate Ganneau's voluminous and highly technical memoirs, to edit the journal and to receive all the visitors—I was married. This event took place in October. Three days before my wedding I received a note from Messrs. Coutts & Co. Two bills had been presented—one from Conder and the other from Ganneau—amounting together to about £300 more than we had in the bank. What was to be done? Most of my people were out of town. One man lent me £50, another £25, I could spare £75, and so on. I went down into the country at last with the comfortable assurance that these bills, at least, would be met. But what was to happen next? My own honeymoon, which I had planned for three weeks, was curtailed to less than a week, and I came back to the empty exchequer with a good deal of anxiety. But the local societies poured in their contributions; the next bills were met; the advances were repaid; and I went on with furnishing a modest semi-detached house at Shepherd's Bush.

The secretaryship of the Palestine Exploration Fund, a small thing which began at £200 a year and after a few years was increased to £300, was the cause—the sole cause—which enabled me to realise my dream of a literary life without dependence, and therefore without degradation. I shall go on in the next chapters to show how I realised that dream. At present I would only note the broad fact that never at anytime was I dependent on my pen for a subsistence. Until my marriage my salary was just sufficient to enable me to live in reasonable comfort. Therefore I was in easy circumstances, comparatively. There was no pressing need for me to write; I could afford to give time to things. Moreover, although my office hours were supposed to be from ten to four, as a rule, except in one or two years, there was not enough work to occupy a quarter of the time. To be sure, visitors came in and wasted the time. But almost everyday I had the greater part of the morning to myself. After the letters had been answered I could carry on my own work in a perfectly quiet office, I could give the afternoon to visitors, and from four till seven I was again free to carry on my work without interruption in my chambers.

I would urge upon everybody who proposes to make a bid for literary success to do so with some backing—a mastership in a school, a Civil Service clerkship, a post as secretary to some institution or society; anything, anything, rather than dependence on the pen, and the pen alone.

IX

First Steps in the Literary Career—and Later

I am going to show in this chapter how I got my feet on the lower rungs of the ladder, and how I began to climb.

I go back to 1868. My book on early French poetry was out and had succeeded among the reviewers. At least I had gained a start and a hearing, and, as I very soon found out, was regarded benevolently by certain editors as a man of some promise. It was in this year that I made the acquaintance of James Rice; he was the editor and proprietor of *Once a Week*. I have already spoken of my voyage to the Island of Réunion, and mentioned the paper I wrote about it. This paper was not acknowledged by the editor, but happening one day to take up *Once a Week* on a railway stall, I found my paper in it—printed badly, uncorrected, and full of mistakes. Naturally I wrote an angry letter, and in reply received a note in very courteous terms inviting me to call. I did so, and learned that the editor had just taken over the paper. He had found my article in type and published it, knowing nothing of the author; he added complimentary remarks on the paper and invited me to write more for him, an invitation which I accepted with much satisfaction.

Next I had an invitation from the late George Bentley, editor of *Temple Bar*, to write for his magazine more studies in French literature. For six or seven years I continued to write papers for this magazine, perhaps three or four every year; towards the end of that time, not so many.

About the year 1870 I was invited to write for the *British Quarterly Review*, to which I contributed some half-a-dozen essays, which cost me a great deal of time and work; among them were papers entitled "The Failure of the French Reformation," "Admiral Coligny," the "Romance of the Rose," and "French Literary Clubs"; and in the year 1871 I wrote a paper for *Macmillan's Magazine* on Rabelais.

In 1870, on the outbreak of the Franco-Prussian War, the Marseillaise was restored to France as its national anthem. I happened to know the history of that hymn and sent a short paper on the subject to the *Daily News*. The editor not only accepted it, but called upon me and asked for more. This led to the contributions of leading articles on social subjects to that paper. I was never on the regular staff, but when I had a subject and could find the time, I would offer an article, and it was seldom that it was refused.

In 1873 I gathered together a group of my various papers and brought them out in volume form called *The French Humorists*.

By this time, then, I was in a position to have as many papers as I could write accepted. I would beg the candidate for literature to consider how it was done:—

1. I was not dependent on literature—I could spend time on my work.
2. I began by producing a book on the subject on which I desired to be considered a specialist. The work had a *succès d'estime*, and in a sense made my literary fortune.
3. This book opened the doors for me of magazines and reviews.
4. The knowledge of French matters also opened the door of the daily press to me.
5. I followed up the line by a second book on the same subject. The press were again, on the whole, very civil.

Circumstances obliged me to give up the pursuit of French literature, but I had at least succeeded in gaining a special reputation and in making an excellent start as a writer on one subject. I was, of course, content with small returns. For my paper on the "Romance of the Rose," which cost me six months and more of solid work, I received £37. Between 1868 and 1873 inclusive, I do not suppose that I ever made so much as £200 a year for all this work. I was, however, unmarried, I lived in chambers, and I still kept my secretaryship. It is really astonishing how well one can live as a bachelor on quite a small income. My rent was £40 a year; my laundress, washing, coals, lights, and breakfast cost me about £70 a year. My dinners—it is a great mistake not to feed well—cost me about thirty shillings a week. Altogether I could live very well indeed on about £250 a year. Practically I spent more, because I travelled whenever I could get away, and bought books, and was fond of good claret. The great thing in literary work is always the same—to be independent: not to worry about money, and not to be compelled to go pot-boiling. I could afford to be anxious about the work and not to be anxious at all about money. And I think that the happiest circumstance of my literary career is that when the money became an object, the money began to come in. While I wanted but little, the income was small.

During this time I was simply making my way alone without any literary acquaintance at all, and quite apart from any literary circles. I have never belonged to any *cénacle*, "school," or Bohemian set. My friends were few: one or two of the old Cambridge lot, a stray Mauritian or two, an old schoolfellow or two. We got up whist in my chambers. I went to the theatre a good deal; to society I certainly did not belong in any sense. And as I was perfectly happy with my private work in my chambers and with such solace of company as offered, I might have continued to the end in this seclusion and solitude, but for the hand of fate, which kindly pulled me out.

My travels at this period were, like my daily life, principally alone. I went about France a good deal—in Normandy, down the Loire, in the unpromising parts of Picardy, about Fontainebleau and across country to Orleans and the neighbourhood. At home I wandered about the Lakes and about Northumberland; visited cathedrals and seaports, watching and observing; I sat in parlours of country inns and listened. The talk of the people, their opinions and their views, amused and interested me. At the time I had no thought of using this material, and so most of it was wasted; but some remained by me.

For a week-end journey I sometimes had a companion in the person of S. L——. He was a barrister without practice, a scholar who neither wrote nor lectured. He read a great deal and had no ambition to reproduce his learning; there was no man of my acquaintance who had a wider knowledge, a better memory, or a sounder critical taste. This critical taste, indeed, he carried into everything; it made him unhappy if his steak at a country inn was not well cooked and well served, and on the important subject of port wine he was really great. Except when he was on one of these journeys he used to get up every afternoon at half-past one, breakfast on coffee and bread and jam—but the jam had to come from his mother's house in the country; at dinner he worked his way through the wine-lists either of club or tavern and always took port after dinner; he would sit in my chambers as late as I allowed him, and he used to go to bed habitually at four. This was his daily life, and he carried it on with the utmost regularity till his death, which happened at the age of fifty-five.

For many years it was my custom to go for a walk in midwinter. My friend Guthrie was my companion in these expeditions. We would be away three or four days, carrying a handbag over the shoulder, taking the train for a convenient distance out of town, and mapping out our walk beforehand so as to give ourselves, if possible, four hours before lunch and about two or three after lunch. Thus I remember a walk we took starting from Newbury, in Wiltshire, to Marlborough, and from Marlborough along the Wans Dyke to Devizes; another from Bath to Glastonbury by way of Radstock, and from Glastonbury to Bridgewater; another from Penzance to Falmouth by way of Helston; and another from Newnham, in Gloucestershire, to Ross, Monmouth, Tintern, and Chepstow—an excellent walk. The exhilaration of such a walk when the weather was frosty and clear cannot be described; the only objection was the long and deadly dulness of the evenings. One got in at about five, dinner was served at seven; what was to be done between seven and ten—the earliest hour at which one could go to bed? There was nothing for it but the smoking-room and the local company, or the billiard-room and the local funny man.

In 1873, in consequence of the publication of *The French Humorists,* I received an invitation to write for the *Saturday Review.* I contributed "middles"—*i.e.*, essays on social matters—to this paper, not regularly, but occasionally, when a good subject came to me. I also reviewed a little for them, but not much. I always disliked reviewing, having an invincible dislike to "slating" an author, or to "log-rolling." I continued to write for the paper till its change of hands in 1894.

In 1871 I brought out the *History of Jerusalem*, the period covered being from the siege by Titus to modern times. Palmer was my *collaborateur*. He contributed the history from Moslem sources which had never before been searched and read for the purpose. I contributed the history as narrated in the Chronicles, which were also nearly new material. The book went out of print, but the sale of the whole edition showed a loss! For many years the book was not to be procured. But it was never dead. At last the publisher consented to issue a second edition subject to the condition of my guarantee of a sale of three hundred copies. To prevent any possible error about this guarantee, I simply took them all at trade price, and put the book in the lists of the Palestine Exploration Fund. The second edition went off at once, and a third edition followed. At the same time I took over from the publisher *The French Humorists*, with the intention of revising, adding to, and improving it for a new edition should the opportunity ever occur.

In 1875—I think—I contributed a volume to Blackwood's Foreign Classics on Rabelais. I also contributed about this time to Blackwood's Series of Foreign Classics, edited by Mrs. Oliphant, a volume on Rabelais. I had a little passage of arms with the editor, who tried to insist that Rabelais, as a Franciscan Friar, had to go about the town *en quête*, begging for the fraternity. She did not understand that long before his time the rule had been crystallised and the practice and custom of the Franciscans modified. The begging of the house simply consisted in the placing of boxes in shops and public places, while the income of the brethren was chiefly made up by Church dues, masses, funerals, and bequests. I followed up the volume with a volume of selections from Rabelais newly translated. I found, however, that it was impossible to make Rabelais popular. The allegorical method appeals to very few, unless the allegory is so simple as to lie quite on the surface. I wrote also a few articles for the *Encyclopædia Britannica*, the most important of which was a paper on Froissart. I wonder if anyone else has ever read Froissart's poems.

In 1873 I joined the Savile Club, then full of young writers, young dons, and young scientific men; but for sometime I hardly used the club at all and was quite unknown to the members. Perhaps to live so retired a life—to spend the evenings alone in solitary chambers, working till eleven o'clock—was a mistake. On the other hand, as I was fated, as it appeared, about this time to write novels, it was just as well to avoid the narrowing influences of the club smoking-room. After my marriage the club smoking-room was farther off than ever, except on Saturdays, when I began to attend the luncheon party and to sit in the circle round the fire afterwards; but always as an occasional guest, never as one of the two or three sets of writers and journalists who belonged to that circle. There was generally very good talk at the Savile: sometimes clever talk, sometimes amusing talk; one always came away pleased, and often with new light on different subjects and new thoughts.

Among the men one met on Saturdays were Palmer, always bubbling over with irrepressible mirth—a school-boy to the end; Charles Leland (Hans Breitmann), full of experiences; Walter Herries Pollock, then the assistant editor of the *Saturday Review*; Gordon Wigan, always ready to personate someone else; Charles Brookfield, as fine a *raconteur* as his father; Edmund Gosse, fast becoming one of the brightest of living talkers; Saintsbury, solid and full of knowledge, a critic to the finger tips, whether of a bottle of port, or a mutton chop, or a poet; H.E. Watts, formerly editor of the *Melbourne Argus*, and translator of *Don Quixote*; Duffield of the broken nose, who also translated *Don Quixote*; Robert Louis Stevenson, then young, and as singularly handsome as he was clever and attractive. Many other of my friends and acquaintances joined the club afterwards, but these are the members most associated in my memory with the Saturday afternoons.

I remember two Saturday afternoons especially. On one of them I had a French novel in my pocket. I had just bought it—a book by the author of *Contes à Ninon*. The circle broke up early, and I began to read the novel. I read it till it was time to go home; I read it in the train; after dinner I read it all the evening. Next day, being Sunday, I read it all the morning and all the afternoon—I finished it in the evening. On Monday, with the magic and the excitement of the story still upon me, I wrote a leading article on the Parisian workman as presented by this book. I took it to the editor of the *Daily News*. He looked it through. "I wish I could take it," he said; "but it is too strong—too strong." I dare say it was too strong, for the book was *L'Assommoir*; but I have always regretted that the article did not appear. The second Saturday afternoon was one spent in reading the proofs of an unpublished story. James Payn sent it to me asking for my opinion. The book was by a new hand. It was called *Vice Versâ*. That was an afternoon to stand out in one's memory.

In 1879–81 I became editor of a series of biographies called, ambitiously, the New Plutarch. Leland gave me a life of Abraham Lincoln; Palmer a life of the Caliph Haroun al Raschid; Conder a life of Judas Maccabæus; and Miss Janet Tucker a life of Joan of Arc. I myself wrote a life of Coligny. Rice undertook the life of Whittington and collected certain notes; but as his illness prevented him from making use of these, I took them over and made the biography a peg for a brief and popular study of mediæval London, putting Rice's name on the title page in acknowledgment of his notes—as I explained in the preface. The series was not successful. After ten years or so I managed to get my two volumes into my own hands again and transferred them to Messrs. Chatto & Windus, where they are still, I believe, alive and in demand. The life of Coligny gave offence to High Church people, but that mattered very little. One can never write anything honest and with conviction without offending someone. I am always pleased to think that I was enabled to present the life of this great man to English readers.

During the last eighteen years or so, I have been chiefly occupied with fiction. In 1885 or thereabouts I found myself unable to discharge the duties of my office at the Palestine Exploration Fund, although they had become very light. I had practically got through with the survey of Western Palestine of which I was director, and my office was continually crowded with editors and publishers and visitors, who came to me not on account of their interest in Palestine. I therefore left off drawing the salary. This left me free to come and go as I liked, and I carried on the correspondence. But this could not last long. The cranks who once had amused me now wasted my time and exasperated me; I had no patience with the multitudes who came with a coin or a lamp. I was compelled to give it up. And so I went out after all into the open without any prop except the money I had made. At the age of fifty, with a big bundle of books and papers behind me, I turned to literature as a profession. But it already gave me an income which would be called handsome even at the bar.

In 1891 I produced the first of four books on London. They were called respectively *London, Westminster, South London*, and *East London*. I shall talk about them and about my London work generally in another chapter.*

I have anticipated events, because it seemed best to keep separate the history of my career as a novelist.

---

* See Chapter XIV. Sir Walter Besant does not, however, mention the four books again.

X

The Start in Fiction: Critics and Criticasters

About 1868 there was a somewhat foolish custom of publishing collections of short stories in Christmas numbers of the magazines. These stories were very poor as a rule, and they were strung together by a quite needless thread. Dickens, for instance, had his *Mugby Function*, the introduction to which he wrote himself. *Once a Week*, of course, must fall in with the fashion. To the Christmas number of 1868 I contributed a short story; to that of 1869 I contributed the larger part. It was called "Titania's Farewell," and described the last night of the fairies in this island. The *motif* was not, it is true, original. Corbett's "Farewell to the Fairies" belonged to the seventeenth century, Wood's "Plea for the Midsummer Fairies" to the nineteenth; but one cannot hope to be always original. The subject was fresh enough for the general reader, and the treatment was light, and I think pleasing, with a slight tinge of sadness. All kinds of bogies, wraiths, and goblins were introduced, and there were dances and songs. In a word, I believe it was a pretty little thing—at all events, it found many friends. It was published anonymously. To me this flimsy trifle became of the utmost importance, because it changed the whole current of my life. In place of a writer of "studies," "appreciations," and the lighter kind of criticism, I became a novelist. Nothing could have been more fortunate. I now understand that there is no branch of the literary life more barren and dreary than that of writing notes upon poets and other writers dead and gone. I have seen the effect of this left upon so many. First, everybody can do it, well or ill; therefore there is a striving for something distinctive, resulting in extravagance, exaggerations, studied obscurity, the pretence of seeing more than other people can see in an author, the parade of an inferior writer as a great genius; so we have the revival of a poet deservedly forgotten—all *pour l'effet*, and all leading directly to habitual dishonesty, sham, and the estimation of form above matter. Indeed, many of these writers of "studies," after a few years, fail to understand matter or to look for anything but form. It is this that they look for and this alone that they talk about. I was rescued from their unfortunate fate while I still clung to the subject-matter as the principal and most important consideration. In an essay the thought is the first thing—the message which the writer has to communicate, the views and conclusions of his mind; the style comes afterwards. A good essay is not an affair of adjectives with new applications, nor of strange phrases, nor of new arrangements of words. At the same time, when a man has a thing to say, he must study how to present it in the most attractive form possible for him.

Consider, for instance, the way of the world in a picture gallery. The crowd go round the rooms from picture to picture; they stop before any canvas that tells a story; they study the story; they do not greatly care for, nor do they inquire too closely into, the method of telling the story—most of them never ask at all how the story is told; they are entirely ignorant about grouping and drawing, about light, shadow, colour, and harmony. Presently the professed critic comes along. Then we hear the art jargon; there is talk of "values," of "middle distance," and all the rest of it; but not a word of instruction. This kind of critic is like the man who writes "studies" and "appreciations": he has developed a jargon. If we are lucky, we may meet the true critic who knows the construction of a picture, and can divine first the thought and attempt of the artist, and next his method, and its success or failure. It is the same with books and their critics. The difference between the sham critic and the real critic is that the latter shows the reader how to look first for the intention of the book and next how to examine into the method employed in carrying out that intention. I do not think that I was born to be a true critic, and by the blessing of the Lord I have been prevented from becoming a sham critic. In the world of letters, I find many who write about books generously and with enthusiasm—these are the young writers; I find many who write jargon—they are mostly the older writers, for the young and generous spirits degenerate; and I find a few, a very few, whose judgments are lessons both to the author and the reader. These true critics are never spiteful; they are never "smart"; they are never derisive; they never pretend to be indignant; they observe courtesy even in condemnation; the writing is always well-bred; and their words are always conclusive.

For my own part I have always belonged to the crowd who read the story in the canvas; and this whether I am studying a picture, a poem, a drama, or a novel. It is the story that I look for first. When I have read, or made out, the story, I may perhaps go on to consider how it is told; perhaps I am quite satisfied with having read the story—indeed, most stories are not worth discussing or considering. In many cases I put the matter first and the form afterwards. The true critic considers the story which the author has attempted to tell, as the first point; the sham critic considers the language and the style (which is, with him, a fashion of the day), and goes no farther. I used to think myself a critic when I was only a sympathetic listener easily absorbed in the story, carried out of myself by the art of the novelist or the poet, whether apparent or concealed. I now understand my limitations in the field of criticism, and I am continually grateful for the accident which took me out of the ranks of reviewers and criticasters and placed me in the company of the story-tellers.

It ought to be understood that a true critic—one who is jealous for both the form and the matter, one who is above all personal considerations, one who is not a "slasher" and a "slater," but a cold and calm judge—is as rare as a true poet, and as valuable. Editors do not understand this. They seem to make no effort to secure the true critics; they allow the disappointed failure, the "slasher," and the "slater" to defile their columns unchecked. There are not, in fact, enough true critics to go round, but an effort should be made by the younger men to imitate their methods. I believe that one can count on ten fingers the few critics whose judgments are lessons of instruction to writers as well as readers, who take broad views of literary work and do not judge a writer by a fault of taste here, or a wrong date there, or an error of opinion, or a mistake in fact.

I was not, I say, by gift of nature one of this small company. Had I continued in the line which I had at first designed, I should certainly have belonged before long to that large company of writers who are always ready with a paper on any literary subject which you like to name; who do odd jobs for publishers; who are made men when they can get a "study" of a writer into a series; and who drag down—down—down—every magazine which gives them free access. In a word, there were two lines open to me: I might continue as secretary of a society and so obtain a livelihood, doing literary work outside the daily hours of routine—always in bachelor chambers, and becoming every year more of a hermit; or I might give up secretarial work and live upon literature—somehow, earning a precarious income, a hack and a dependent, soured, poor, disappointed, and bitter. There are many such unfortunates about. They pretend to be leaders; they give themselves airs of superiority; they are bitter and ungenerous reviewers; their lot is still the lot of Grub Street; they are, as always, the children of Gibeon who hew wood and draw water and do hack work for their employers, for the pay of a solicitor's clerk. That I was spared from taking either of these two obvious lines was greatly due to the writing and publishing of "Titania's Farewell."

For after the appearance of "Titania's Farewell," Rice came to me with a proposal. It was that I would collaborate with him in writing a novel, the plot of which had already been drawn out in the rough by himself. His plot was simply the story of the Prodigal Son with variations. The wanderer was to return apparently repentant, in reality resolved upon getting out of the old man all that he could secure. The father was to be a rich miser, a banker in a country town. The idea seemed to offer great possibilities in the way of incident and character. In fact, the more one looked at it, the more these possibilities extended. Of course the Prodigal would have a past to hamper him; one past belonging to the time before he left the paternal home, and another belonging to his adventurous career about the world. I accepted the proposal. I set to work with a will, and before long our Prodigal was working out his later developments in the columns of *Once a Week*. The plot, naturally, was modified. The Prodigal grew more human; he became softened; but the past remained with him to hamper him and to drag him down.

When it came to reproducing the story as a volume, Rice proposed that we should print it and give it to a publisher as a commission book. There was no doubt about its success from the first. As a pecuniary speculation it was as successful as could be expected in those days, when half-a-dozen novelists commanded a circulation in three-volume forms of twelve hundred or so; and the next dozen or so were lucky if they got rid of six hundred copies of their works. I do not think that my own share of the proceeds, from the beginning to the end, of *Ready Money Mortiboy* reached more than £200 or £250.

I have often been asked to explain the method of collaboration adopted by Rice and myself. The results were certainly satisfactory so far as popularity was concerned, a fact which goes a long way to explaining this curiosity, no other literary collaboration having been comparable, in this country, with ours for success. My answer to the question was always the same. It is impossible that I should offer any explanation or give any account of this method, seeing that my *collaborateur* has been dead since the year 1882. It is enough to state that we worked without disagreement; that there was never any partnership between us in the ordinary sense of the word; but that the collaboration went on from one story to another always without any binding conditions, always liable to be discontinued; while each man carried on his own independent literary work, and was free to write fiction, if he pleased, by himself.

The collaboration had its advantages; among others, that of freeing me, for my part, from the worry of business arrangements. I am, and always have been, extremely averse from making terms and arrangements for myself. At the same time, if I were asked for my opinion as to collaboration in fiction, it would be decidedly against it. I say this without the least desire to depreciate the literary ability of my friend and *collaborateur*. The arrangement lasted for ten years and resulted in as many successful novels. I only mean that, after all, an artist must necessarily stand alone. If two men work together, the result must inevitably bear the appearance of one man's work; the style must be the same throughout; the two men must be rolled into one; each must be loyal to the other; neither can be held responsible for plot, incident, character, or dialogue. There will come a time when both men fret under the condition; when each desires, but is not able, to enjoy the reputation of his own good work; and feels, with the jealousy natural to an artist, irritated by the loss of half of himself and ready to accept the responsibility of failure in order to make sure of the meed of success. Now that Rice is dead it is impossible for me to lay hands upon any passage or page and to say "This belongs to Rice—this is mine." The collaboration would have broken down, I believe, amicably. It would have been far better if it had broken down five years before the death of Rice, so that he might have achieved what has been granted to myself— an independent literary position.

There are, however, some parts in our joint work which, without injustice to him or to myself, I may fairly assign to one or the other. In *Ready Money Mortiboy*, as I have stated, the plot and the origin and the conception were his; the whole of the part concerned with the country town and the bank is his. On the other hand, in the story called *By Celia's Arbour* the whole of the local part, that which belongs to Portsmouth, is my own. I was born in the place, which Rice never, to my knowledge, even saw. On the other hand, there are many parts of all the stories, in which our rambles about London, and conversations over these rambles, suggested situations, plots, and characters, which it would be impossible to assign to either. Of *The Golden Butterfly*, the origin which has already been plainly stated in certain introductions may be repeated. The thing itself—the Golden Butterfly—was seen by my brother, Mr. Edgar Besant, in Sacramento, California. He told me about it, and it suggested possibilities. Rice at the same time had thought of a story of a Canadian who "struck ile," became a millionaire, created a town, and was there ruined, town and all, by the drying up of the supply. He also found the "fighting editor." The twins were a reminiscence, not an invention, of my own. The rest, as any novelist will understand, was simply the construction of a novel with these materials as its basis. This story appeared in the year 1876, a quarter of a century ago. Like *Ready Money Mortiboy*, it has never ceased to sell: last year the publishers—now the proprietors—brought out an edition at sixpence. They sold the whole—150,000 copies—in three weeks. I repeat that I desire to suggest nothing that might seem to lessen the work of Rice in the collaboration, while, both for his sake and my own, I regret that it ever went beyond *The Golden Butterfly*, which was quite the most successful of the joint novels. The continued popularity of this and one or two others of my novels has always been the most gratifying circumstance in my literary career.

In 1876 Rice and I began to write the Christmas number for *All the Year Round*, which was continued until Rice's death in 1882, and after that by myself till 1887. The stories which formed these Christmas numbers were in length very nearly as long as many stories now produced at six shillings. Some of them were very popular; all of them gave me the greatest pleasure possible in writing, partly because they were short enough to turn on a single *motif* with a small number of characters. The three-volume novel, on the other hand, was three times the length of the Christmas number and presented much greater constructive difficulties. The ignorant reviewer used to talk of the "Procrustean" length of the three-volume novel. Of course there was no more uniformity of length about the three-volume novel than exists now with the one-volume. The three-volume novel, in fact, varied in length, say, from 100,000 words to 300,000 words. It was thought to be giving short measure to present the former length, but the longer might tax the energies of the reader too much.

The ignorant reviewer has also, on many occasions, waxed eloquent over the estimate of length by so many words. He imagines that the words are carefully counted and that the writer is bound not to exceed a certain fixed number and not to offer a story less than that number. Now, since most novels of repute appear first as serials, one is bound to consider the length of each instalment, and there is no more ready way of estimating the length than by the number of words. I have written serials for a great many publications. Let me take one, the *Illustrated London News*. Here the only condition imposed on the author was that the story was to run for twenty-six weeks. This meant an average length of so many columns. Translated into numbers, it meant about 6,000 words for each instalment. But I am quite certain that the editor of the *Illustrated London News* never counted the words; if the chapter was a few hundred words over or under the average length, it mattered nothing. As I always write on paper of the same size and know very approximately the number of words that fill one page, I have never had any difficulty in dividing the chapters into tolerably equal instalments.

Formerly, the writer reckoned by sheets; still he must have learned how many words go to a sheet; or by pages, but still he must have learned how many words go to a page; or by columns, but with the same necessity. It is surely better to begin at once with the number of words, always understanding that there is not, as the ignorant reviewer would insist, a yard measure or a two-foot rule introduced or any rigid condition about the number of words.

Let me note one or two other points on which the reviewer often betrays his ignorance. The *Spectator* is in most respects a well-conducted and well-informed journal. I saw in the *Spectator* sometime ago a notice of a certain recently deceased writer who, the reviewer pointed out, had most unfortunately brought out his novels in serial form, so that he was compelled to end each instalment with a sensational incident, a circumstance which spoiled his work. One would really think that a person allowed to write for the *Spectator* would have known better than to talk such rubbish; he or she would at least, one would think, have sufficient knowledge of the history of fiction to know that Dickens, Thackeray, Trollope, George Eliot, Charles Reade, Wilkie Collins, George Meredith, William Black, Blackmore, Hardy—everybody of note among modern novelists—brought out their novels in serial form. Yet this fact has not spoiled their work. I have, if that affects the question, brought out nearly all my novels in serial form first. And I may safely aver that I have never felt, recognised, or understood that there was the least necessity for ending an instalment with an incident. There is, however, no end to the rubbish—mostly ignorant, partly malevolent—that is written and published about novels. In the same paper, for instance, I found the other day an objection to one of my characters on the ground that it was not a "transcript from nature!" Therefore, if you please, no novelist has a right to present a character which is not a portrait! Why, the characters of the first and best novelists are never "transcripts" from nature. They are suggested by certain points, often unsuspected points, in real characters. That to which my reviewer objected was a character suited to the actual times, insomuch as he might very well exist, and perhaps does exist. No impossibility was presented. But he was certainly not a "transcript from nature."

The ignorant and prejudiced reviewer of novels is not perhaps so much to blame as the editor of the paper where the review appears, for so long as the editor expects his reviewer to pronounce a judgment upon a dozen novels every week, so long will those judgments be either miserably inadequate or dishonest. I cannot conceive any kind of work more demoralising to a writer than that of reviewing a dozen novels every week in, say, two columns. The inevitable result is that he loses all sense of proportion; one novel becomes as much worth mentioning as another; George Meredith—as actually happened once in a "literary" journal—may be dismissed in a paragraph between the works of two schoolgirls. The reviewer, after a short course of this kind of work, loses the power of judgment; he scamps the reading so persistently that he becomes unable to read; he makes an effort to get at something like the story, which he proceeds to tell baldly and badly; appreciation is impossible where there has been no real reading: he cannot praise because praise is a definite thing which, unless it is general and meaningless, must be based on actual reading; but he can depreciate. Sometimes, of course, in his haste, he makes dire blunders. I have known many such cases. Thus, a novel praised to the skies one week was slated pitilessly, a few weeks later, *in the same weekly*! I remember once in the *Athenæum* a notice of a novel of my own. The book was dismissed in eight or ten lines, everyone of which contained a separate misstatement concerning the story. It was, I remember, stated that the whole action of the book took place in a banker's office. There was no mention of such a thing as a bank or a banker in the whole book.

It is to me, I confess, a continual subject of wonder that an editor who allows books to be noticed in batches—ten or a dozen every week—does not understand that by doing so he actually throws away the whole weight of his paper as a critical organ—the whole weight of his authority. Surely it would be better, in the long run, to preserve the character of a paper for fair, dispassionate, and competent criticism, than, for the sake of pleasing publishers (who are wholly indifferent to criticism and care for nothing at all but a line of praise that they can quote, to issue miserable little paragraphs, whose praise carries no conviction—because it is and must be, so long as the present plan of reviewing by batches continues, couched in general terms—and whose condemnation can produce no effect upon the mind of the reader. Yet, in one paper after another, the suicidal policy is preserved. It must be remembered that these paragraphs are simply passed over by the majority of readers. It is impossible, week after week, to persuade them that the batch of books so noticed can have been read.

Another point in which the ordinary editor is blameworthy is that he takes no care to keep out of his paper the personal element. He allows the log-roller to praise his own friends and the spiteful and envious failure to abuse his enemies. This carelessness is so common in English journalism that one knows beforehand, when certain books appear, the organs in which they will be praised or assailed. Surely, for the credit of his paper, an editor might at least ascertain, beforehand, that a critic is neither the friend nor the enemy of the author. In the *New York Critic*, I have been told, every reviewer is on his honour not to undertake a criticism of the work of a personal friend or a personal enemy. We have many things to learn from America. The maintenance of the honour and the reputation and the authority of the critical columns of our journals is one of these things.

It is, of course, quite impossible for any journal to deal with all the books that appear—the trashy novels especially. Surely a review should be a distinction for the author and an opportunity for the critic. Why should not a responsible paper select one or two novels a week, as worthy, not of a paragraph among a batch of other paragraphs, but of a serious review by someone who is competent to speak of a work of art? There are certainly not a hundred novels in the year which are really so worthy; and the judgment, calmly considered, by a serious and educated critic should not only be of service to the author and to the book, but it would be instructive to the reader, who has for the most part studied no canons of criticism and formed consciously no literary standards. But the reviewer must be serious and educated. He must know what the canons of criticism mean; he must be trustworthy; he must not be the hack who rolls the log for his friend and "slates" his enemies; he must be in a word, a man of honour. Should there, then, be no criticism of bad books? Assuredly. It is a foolish waste of time and space to "slate" a poor little weakling which will never be presented to the public except in a seaside circulating library, made up of "remainders." But in the case of a bad book, or a mischievous book, or a book which has succeeded and yet ought not to have succeeded, it is the duty of the critic to inform and instruct the reader as to the true character and tendencies of this book. This he can very well do, if he is himself a gentleman as well as a scholar, in the language and the manner of courtesy and politeness.

Let me return to my subject. The collaboration between Rice and myself lasted for one book after another—there was never any binding agreement, contract, or partnership—for about ten years. During this time we produced three highly successful novels, viz., *Ready Money Mortiboy*, *The Golden Butterfly*, and *The Chaplain of the Fleet*, and others— *My Little Girl*, *By Celia's Arbour*, *This Son of Vulcan*, *With Harp and Crown*, *The Monks of Thelema*, *The Seamy Side*, and two or three volumes of short stories, including *The Case of Mr. Lucraft*, all of which did very well and made friends for the writers. The method of publication pursued was simple. The novel or the story first appeared in a magazine or journal; it was then published in three-volume form; after a year or so it came out in a single volume at 3s. 6d.; and finally as a "yellow-back" at 2s.

I think, trying to put myself outside these novels, that they are really a collection with which one may reasonably be satisfied. The book that I like best of them all is *The Chaplain of the Fleet*. It was the first of my eighteenth-century novels, and perhaps the best. The situations, the plot, the characters, all seem to me, if I may speak in praise of myself, original and striking. It was a subject which lent itself to firm and vigorous drawing. I am, in fact, more and more convinced that the first and most important thing is to have a clear story with strong characters. It was impossible that reviewers could be more appreciative than those who reviewed this series of novels. The collaboration lasted off and on for ten years. Then it came to an end.

Early in 1881 Rice was attacked by an illness, for which he came to town, thinking that a week or two of rest and treatment would set him right. He stayed in town for six weeks; he then went home and reported himself in a fair way of recovery. But then followed symptoms which were persistent and unaccountable; he could not eat anything without suffering dire pains; he tried oysters, chopped up raw beef, all kinds of things. Then the pains vanished; he even thought himself quite recovered; he went for a week or two to Dunquerque in August. On his return the symptoms reappeared. After lingering for six months in great suffering, he died in April 1882 at the age of thirty-nine; the cause was a cancer in the throat.

XI

The Novelist with a Free Hand

My life between 1882 and 1900 is a simple chronicle of work done. Perhaps it may be of no interest to my readers. In that case let the chapter be omitted, because it is purely personal. During this period my beard grew grey; I advanced from forty-six to sixty-four; from middle age I became old; but I never ceased to rejoice in my work; to find every novel—there was one a year—the most delightful I had ever written; to fall in love with my heroine; to admire my young men of virtue; and to desire, above all things, that my villain should reap the fruit of his iniquities. Thus are we made. When villainies are exposed, we desire nothing so much as the performer's punishment; no punishment can be too severe for so great a villain; we burn to see him scourged. Yet we never wax in the least indignant over our own meannesses and frailties—call them not villainies, though their fruits may be as poisonous as the monstrous growths that follow the crimes of fiction.

Eighteen novels in eighteen years! It seems a long list; how can one write so much and yet survive? My friends, may I ask why a painter is allowed to produce a couple of pictures and more every year and no one cries out upon him for his haste in production; yet if a story-teller gives to the world a novel every year, the criticaster yaps at his heels and asks all the world to observe the haste which the novelist makes to get rich. Poor novelist! It is not often, indeed, that he does get rich. In my own case I was endowed by nature with one quality which, I am sure, I may proclaim without boasting. It is that of untiring industry. It is no merit in me to work continuously. I am not happy when I am not working. I cannot waste the afternoon in a club smoking-room; nor can I waste two hours before dinner in a club library; nor can I waste a whole morning pottering about a garden; and in the evening, after dinner, I am fain to repair to my study, there to look over proofs, hunt up points, and arrange for the next day's work. Again, when I have fiction in hand I cannot do any good with it for more than three or four hours a day—say from nine till half-past twelve. In the afternoon I must work at other things. What those things have been, I will speak of presently.

I find that, on an average, a novel has taken me about eight or ten months from the commencement to the end. If you turn this statement into a little sum in arithmetic, you will find that it means about a thousand words a day. Do not, however, imagine that I write a thousand words a day. Not at all. My method (again advising readers not interested in this confession to go on to the next chapter) always has been the same. The central *motif* of the story is first settled and decided upon. It should be a plain, clear, and intelligible *motif*—one which all the world can understand. Round this theme has to be grouped a collection of characters whose actions, conversations, and motives form a clear and consistent story while they supply views of life, pictures of life, and illustrations of life. It is obvious that to find these characters is the great difficulty; it is obvious that one may easily fall into mistakes and decide upon characters without much interest to the reader. Now the writer does not understand this until too late. I could name one of my stories where the central theme was very good and should have been striking, but the tale was marred by the lack of interest in the principal character.

However, the *motif*, the story, and the characters having been decided upon, the next step is the presentation, which involves practice and study in the art of construction. I would not insist too strongly on the study required for the construction of a story, because if an aspirant has not the gift, no study will endow him with it. But he should certainly pay great attention at the outset. Above all, he should aim at presenting his situations with a view to dramatic effect; not, that is, to let down the curtain at the end of a chapter upon a *tableau*, but to lead up to the situation dramatically, to present it dramatically, and to group his characters, so to speak, dramatically. He should also avoid long descriptions of character; very few writers can do these well; it is best for the ordinary novelist to make his characters describe themselves in dialogue. This is easy, provided that the writer has got a clear grip of each character and can make him talk, without effort, up to his character. He will, of course, have an eye to proportion. It is amazing to find how many novels are ruined for want of due proportion between the parts, so that the beginning overshadows the end, or the end is out of harmony with the beginning.

For my own part, I proceed, after the preliminaries, which generally take three weeks or a month of irritating experiment, failure, and patient trying over and over again, to write at headlong speed the first two or three chapters. These I lay aside for a few days and then take them up again; the heat of composition is over and one can then estimate in cold blood what the thing means and how it promises. In any case, it has all to be written over again: the first draft is chaotic; the dialogue is only suggested; the situations are slurred; things irrelevant or of no consequence are introduced. Then I set to work to rewrite, to correct, and to expand. Very often the first rough chapter becomes an introduction, followed by two or three chapters which begin the story. At the same time I go on to another rough draft of future chapters. So the novel is constructed much on the principle of a tunnel, in which the rough boring and blasting goes on ahead, while the completion of the work slowly follows. After a little there is no longer the least trouble about quantity of material; it becomes solely a question of selection; the characters are all alive and they are working out the story in their own way—there are sometimes a dozen situations from which one only can be chosen—and their talk is incessant and, for the most part, wide of the mark—that is to say, it interests them but it does not advance the story. And so the time passes; the summer follows the spring; the novelist is absorbed almost everyday for three or four hours with his work. Unless he is working at other things he lives in a dream; he does not want to talk much; he does not want society; he wants only to be left alone. To dream away one's life is pleasant; but alas! no one knows how swiftly the time passes in a dream. For thirty years I have been dreaming during the greater part of every year. What should I have done had it not been for this pageant of Dreamland, which has kept me perfectly happy, though sometimes careless and oblivious of the outer world?

Perhaps it is superfluous to describe the methods of my work; as I said before, my readers may pass over this chapter; it may, however, be of some use to young aspirants to know how a craftsman in their art worked—may I add?—*non sine gloriâ*, not without a certain measure of success.

I do not propose to describe the genesis of these novels, or to relate the chronicles of small beer about their production, the opinions of the press upon them, and their pecuniary returns. I have stated my general method of writing a novel; not, mind, so many pages, or so many hours a day; not sitting down by a blind rule, nor waiting till the inspiration came—that is only another name for prolonged idleness under a nonsensical pretence; but I exercised upon myself a certain amount of pressure at the outset, when the work was difficult and the way thorny; and afterwards, when the way was easy I sat down morning after morning unless indisposition, or some engagement which must be kept, forbade. As to the appearance of these novels, they all came out in serial form simultaneously in America as well as in England. Let me here express my great and lasting gratitude to my agents, Mr. A.P. Watt and his son, by whose watch and ward my interests have been so carefully guarded for eighteen years. During that time I have always been engaged for three years in advance; I have been relieved from every kind of pecuniary anxiety; my income has been multiplied by three at least; and I have had, through them, the offer of a great deal more work than I could undertake. I cannot speak too strongly of the services rendered to me by my literary agents. Of course, there are different kinds of agents. There is the agent, for example, who knows nothing about his business. But the agent who does know his business, who knows also editors, publishers, and their arrangements, may be of immense use to the novelist, the essayist, the traveller—in short, to the author of any book that can command a circulation and a public demand.

And such an agent is Mr. A.P. Watt.

Of the eighteen novels, by far the best, in my own judgment, is *Dorothy Forster*. It was, I think, in 1869 that I first visited what is perhaps the most interesting county in the whole of England—Northumberland. It was in Bamborough Castle that I first heard the story of Dorothy Forster. It occurred to me then, before I had begun to think of becoming a novelist, that the story was a subject which presented great possibilities; but as yet I had only written one story, which was a failure. In 1874 I was married. I had by that time written certain novels which had some success, and I had already resolved vaguely upon undertaking the subject as soon as I could find time and opportunity. After my marriage I made the very interesting discovery that my wife's family had changed their name in the year 1698, or thereabouts, from Forster to Barham; that they were descendants of the Forsters of Addlestone and Bamborough, through Chief Justice Forster of Queen Elizabeth's time, and that Dorothy Forster, my heroine, was therefore my wife's cousin, though ever so many times removed. This was, I say, a very interesting discovery. We went down to Bamborough a year or two later, making a pilgrimage to the old home. In 1880 or 1881 I went again by myself, the purpose of writing the book having grown more definite. I visited all the places that I wanted for the story, and made many notes as to the local surroundings. In 1882 I took my father-in-law with me, and we made together a posting-tour of the country. This is quite the best way to see the country-side, and I really think that I have seen nearly the whole of Northumberland—not quite all, but the most important part—in these four visits. In 1883 I wrote the story—with great ease, because it was already in my head—and in 1884 it came out in the *Graphic*, being most beautifully illustrated by my late friend, Charles Green, whose drawing, to my mind, was surpassed by few, while his conscientious care in the selection of the most telling situations and in draping his models with correct costumes was beyond all praise. He gave me three or four of the drawings, which I had framed. They now hang on my staircase, where I can see them everyday, and so be reminded of Dorothy, of Northumberland, and of Charles Green. The book dealt with the Rebellion of 1715, but in its side issues. I leave battle-pieces to any who choose; I know my own limitations, which do not include exercises in military strategy. A battle is beyond me; the marching and the charging and the points of vantage confuse me. So also courts and grandeurs are beyond me. But I had my brave and loving Dorothy with me. All through the book, in every chapter and on every page, I loved her and I let her talk and act; to be with her was better from my point of view than the clang and clash of a dozen battles.

Four other stories out of the eighteen also belonged to the eighteenth century. They were *For Faith and Freedom* (end of seventeenth century), *The World Went Very Well Then*, *St. Katherine's by the Tower*, and *The Orange Girl*.* The first of these, like *Dorothy Forster*, was a story showing how a great rebellion, that of Monmouth's, affected the fortunes of a small group. The battle of Sedgemoor, the, *haute politique*, the intrigues of the Court, belonged to another novel, unwritten. Mine had to do with the by-ways, the side-currents, the backwater of that movement. Conan Doyle brought out his novel of *Micah Clarke* at the same time and on the same subject. I do not think the two stories injured each other.

One anecdote in connection with this story illustrates the "long arm of coincidence." The people in my novel were sent out to Barbadoes as political convicts. I desired above all things to follow them there. Indeed, it was necessary unless a great opportunity should be thrown

---

* *The Lady of Lynn*, which was in the press when its author died, is also an eighteenth-century story.

away. But I could find nothing on the subject. Defoe, it is true, talked about Virginia and the Plantations, and in his own manner, apparently, gave exact details. When, however, one looked into the pages, the exact details were only there in appearance—he did not know the daily life. Now I wanted everything: the hours of work, the kind of work, the dress, the food, the treatment of the prisoners by the overseers—everything. What was I to do? I went to the British Museum: nothing seemed known. I became sorrowfully aware that I should have to invent the details, or to guess at them from the very meagre notes at my disposal. Now to me, pondering sadly on this necessity, there came one evening half-a-dozen catalogues of second-hand books. I turned them over idly, marking such books as seemed likely to be of help in the restoration of the past, when suddenly I came upon a title that made me jump. It was "The Journal of A. B——, sometime chyrurgeon to the Duke of Monmouth, with his trial and sentence to the Plantations of Barbadoes; his Captivity there; and his Escape. Price, One Guinea." Heavens! What luck! For here was the very thing I wanted! In the morning I drove off early to the bookseller's. The book was gone! An American had picked it up the day before. But I had at least the title, and, armed with this, I went off again to the British Museum. In the vast ocean of pamphlets in the library this was found. I caused the whole thing to be copied out bodily, with the result that I had a chapter charged with real life, and with the actualities of convict labour in the late seventeenth century. Needless to say that none of my reviewers noticed this chapter. One man to whom I told the story coldly observed, "Then you stole that chapter." Why, a man who writes a novel of past life, as a history of past life, must steal—if you call it so! He may invent, but then it will not be past life; he must use the old material if he can find it; if he cannot find it, he cannot write a novel of past life.

The third story of the past is called *The World Went Very Well Then*. The leading incident round which the story is constructed was, in like manner, found by me. About the end of the seventeenth century there was a certain young lieutenant of the Navy, who promised a girl at Deptford marriage when he should return from his next cruise. He did return; she reminded him of his promise; he laughed at her. She fell on her knees and prayed solemnly that God Almighty would smite him in that part which he should feel the most. He was then appointed captain of a ship. He took her into action, having the reputation of a brave and gallant officer. He was seized with sudden cowardice and struck the flag at the first shot. That was my material for the story, and very good material it was. The story came out in the *Illustrated London News*, and was admirably illustrated by Mr. Forestier.

Another eighteenth-century story, suggested by an incident of the time, was *St. Katherine's by the Tower*. In this story the young suitor comes home to marry his sweetheart. He arrives full of love and of happiness. To his amazement the girl shrinks from him, rejects him, with every sign of loathing and disgust. More than this, she falls into melancholia, threatening decline. The lover thinks that his death alone will cause her recovery. He courts death in many ways, but death avoids him. He therefore joins a company of so-called "traitors," and is sentenced to death. The rest of the story may be found in the pages of the book.

Of the other novels I must speak very briefly. They are either studies of the East End and of the people, as *All Sorts and Conditions of Men, The Children of Gibeon, The Alabaster Box*—a story of a settlement—and *The Rebel Queen*, or they are stories of today. *All in a Garden Fair* presents an account, somewhat embroidered, of my own literary beginnings. *Herr Paulus* is a story of spiritualistic fraud—I have always rejoiced to think that the story was considered a great blow to Sludge and his friends. *Armorel of Lyonesse* is an exposure of the impudent charlatan who produces artistic and literary works under his own name which are executed by another's hand—a fraud more common, I have been told, ten years ago, than it is now. *The City of Refuge* is a story of life in one of the American communities. *The Master Craftsman* is the history of the politician who makes himself by the aid of an ambitious woman. *Beyond the Dreams of Avarice* is a tale of the evil influence of the inheritance of great wealth. Of course such a theme easily brings to the stage a number of people of all kinds and all conditions. The prospect of wealth corrupts and demoralises everyone—the man of science, the man of pleasure, the colonial, the actor, the American.

The Fourth Generation is the most serious of all my novels. Here we have to deal with the truth that the children do undoubtedly suffer for the sins of the fathers. It is impossible to deny the facts of the case; they are conspicuous in every family, in all history. It seems unjust. The Hebrew Prophets considered the case; one of them proclaimed the law; another defined its limitation. In the novel I have admitted the law. I have shown how, by reason of an undetected crime, one member of a family after another is struck with misfortune and degraded by crimes. Yet there are the limitations. A reviewer, in speaking in commendation of the story, said that he was amazed to find a reference to a Hebrew Prophet in the preface. The amazement was caused by his inability to understand that a novel may be a perfectly serious document and that a novelist may illustrate a most important law of humanity by a simple, even an amusing, story. The limitations are plainly laid down by the Prophet Ezekiel. They amount to this: The father, by his sins, may condemn his children for many generations to poverty, to the loss of social position, to the loss of all the advantages to which they were born; he may reduce them all to servitude; he may make it impossible for them to retrieve their former position, so that they can neither get oblivion of the past nor make a new beginning on the foundation of the old evils. But he cannot touch the souls of his children. "As I live, saith the Lord God"—hear the Prophet's more than solemn words—"the soul of every man is mine." If the children commit sins and crimes, they will make it still harder for *their* descendants, but the crimes are not caused by the sins of the fathers. "Amazing," said my reviewer.

When I read the criticasters' paragraphs about novels "with a purpose," I ask myself what novel I have written that had not a purpose. Among my shorter stories *Katherine Regina*, the most successful, shows the misery of being left destitute without special training or knowledge. *The Inner House* is an allegory in which it is shown that everything worth having in life depends upon death, the appointed end. One reviewer said it was an attack on socialism. Twenty others immediately followed suit, glad of a chance of noticing without reading. *In Deacon's Orders* is a study in religiosity, which is an emotion quite apart from religion.

The Revolt of Man I brought out anonymously. It shows the world turned upside down. Women rule everything and do the whole of the intellectual work; the Perfect Woman is worshipped instead of the Perfect Man. The reception of the book was at first extremely cold; none of the reviews noticed it except slightingly; it seemed as if it was going to fail absolutely. Then an article in the *Saturday Review*, written in absolute ignorance of the authorship, started all the papers. I sent for my friend the editor to lunch with me, and confessed the truth. In five or six weeks we had got through about nine thousand copies. When I say that the advanced woman has never ceased to abuse the book and the author, its success will be understood.

My course as a novelist—or anything else—is now nearly finished. I do not suppose I can, even in the few years or weeks that may be left to me, do anything so good as the work that lies behind. But of all forms of work, there is none, to me at least, which could possibly be more delightful than that of fiction. One never wearies of the work; it fills the brain with groups of people, all curious and all interesting, some most charming and some most villainous. I have never attempted what is called analysis of character. Most so-called "analyses" of character are mere laborious talks—attempts to do on many pages what should be done in single strokes and in easy dialogue. If my people do not reveal themselves by their acts and words, then I have failed. But, character is complex? Quite so; the most complex character can only be understood by acts and words. The analysers start with a view of art which is not mine. I admit, however, that in the hands of one or two writers the results have been very fine. But it is not the art of Fielding, Smollett, Scott, Thackeray, Dickens, Reade. With all these writers the analysis of character takes the form of presentation of character by act and word. At the outset, all we know of a person in the tale is that he has done certain things. Then, by degrees, perhaps without the knowledge or the intention of the writer, the character talks and acts in such a way, under the influence of conditions of birth, education, and surroundings, as to make us understand how complex is his character, how strangely mixed of good and evil. And this kind of art seems to me by far the higher and the truer, and to give better results, simply because no writer is able at the outset to say, "Thus and thus shall be the character of my hero; so complex; shot with so many hues; so full of changes and surprises; so shifting and so blown about here and there by every wind that sweeps his level." For my own part I like my characters to tread the stage speaking and acting so that all the world may understand them and their revelation of themselves in works and ways, in thoughts and speech. Mine, it will be objected, is a simple form of art. Is it not, however, the art of Dickens, Scott, and Fielding? Let me belong to the school of the Masters; let me be content to follow humbly and at however great a distance in the lines laid down by them.

To return to my work. "Why do you not give us," said one to me, "the fun and laughter of *The Golden Butterfly*?" Well, you see, I was in my thirties then, and I am now in my sixties. The bubbling spirits of a sanguine and cheerful temperament made me happy and made of the world a Garden of Delight in those days. The spirits which enabled me to contribute to the cheerfulness of my readers when that book and certain other of my collaborations were written are gone. They cannot exist with my present time of life. What is left me is at best but a sobered cheerfulness. Yet, I think, my work has never yet been gloomy. Thank Heaven! I have had less during my life, so far, to make me gloomy in the sixties than falls to the lot of many men in the thirties. Let me, in what remains of life, preserve cheerfulness, if only the cheerfulness of common gratitude. No one ought to acknowledge more profoundly than myself the happiness that has been bestowed upon me; the domestic peace; the freedom from pecuniary troubles; literary success in a measure unhoped for; a name known all over the English-speaking world; and circles of friends. And with them a whole army of enemies—exactly such enemies as one, at the outset, would desire above all things, to make: the spiritualistic fraud with his lying pretensions and his revelations revealing nothing from the other world; the sickly sentimentalist blubbering over the righteous punishment of the sturdy rogue; and the shrieking sisterhood. They are all my enemies, and if, at the beginning of life, I had been asked what enemies I would make—could I have made a better choice?

XII*

The Society of Authors and Other Societies

It was in the month of September and the year 1883 that a small company of twelve or fifteen men met in Mr. Scoones's chambers, Garrick Street, in order to form an association or society of men and women engaged in letters. What we were going to do; how we were going to do anything; what was wanted; why it was wanted—all these things were not only imperfectly understood, they were not understood at all. It was only felt vaguely, as it had been felt for fifty years, that the position of literary men was most unsatisfactory. The air was full of discontent and murmurs; yet when any broke out into open accusation, the grievance, in some mysterious way, became insubstantial, and the charge, whatever it was, fell to the ground. It was impossible to find a remedy, because the disease itself could not be diagnosed. Nevertheless the murmuring continued, and either rolled about the air in harmless thunder or broke out into epigrams. The discontent of authors may be traced back for a hundred and fifty years simply by the continuous beaded string of epigrams in which they have relieved their angry souls.

We began, therefore, in our ignorance, with one or two quite safe general propositions. Nothing could be more simple, more unpretending, or more innocent than the general propositions of the Society. We proposed, in short, three objects: (1) The maintenance, definition, and defence of literary property; (2) the consolidation and amendment of the laws of domestic copyright; (3) the promotion of international copyright.

---

* Sir Walter Besant, in a note at the end of the ninth chapter of his manuscript, refers to his intention to tell the story of the Society of Authors, and later alludes to the Society as though he had fulfilled this design. The account of the Society of Authors which follows was written in 1892, and was read by him at the annual meeting of that year, on his resignation of the chairmanship. Undoubtedly this is the account which he meant to include in his autobiography, though he would have made corrections and additions, most of which are called for by the lapse of ten years. All that Sir Walter Besant said is not included, for some of his words were due to the occasion, and had no direct bearing on the story of the Society in which he was so profoundly interested.

This statement or announcement of intention, it was hoped, would give no offence and excite no jealousies. We were naturally, at the outset, distrustful of ourselves; uncertain as to the support we should receive; timid as to our power of doing anything at all; anxious not to do mischief. Later experience has partly removed this timidity. We have ventured, and shall now continue, to speak openly and to publish and proclaim aloud the whole truth connected with the literary profession.

Fortunately, we discovered very early in our proceedings that even a document so modest as our first circular was giving dire offence in certain quarters. It was more than hinted that the results to all concerned would be disastrous to the last degree. That was nine years ago. What things have been said and done since that time! Yet here we stand, not a whit the worse, any of us; and how much better we are now going to consider. I say that this was a fortunate discovery, because it showed us that we should encounter opposition whatever we might do or say. Literary property, we were given to understand quite clearly, was to be considered as a sacred ark which none but the priests—*i.e.*, those who had it already in their hands—might touch. This opposition in some quarters took the form of personal appeals to authors not to join the new association, while in many cases the fear of giving offence and suffering loss in consequence caused—and even still causes—some to hold aloof.

Having, then, produced our prospectus, we set to work to gain the adhesion of as many leaders in literature as we could. Our first and greatest success—a success which won for us at the outset respectful consideration—was the acceptance by Lord Tennyson of the presidency. Had we elected, or been compelled to accept, any lesser man than the Laureate, our progress would have been far more difficult. With him at our head we were from the first accepted seriously.

Our next success lay in the extremely respectable and representative body of members who consented to join us as our vice-presidents. As a representative body, no list could have been more gratifying. Poetry was represented—to name only a few—by the second Lord Lytton, Sir Theodore Martin, and Matthew Arnold; science by Huxley, Lord Rayleigh, Michael Foster, Tyndall, Norman Lockyer, Sir Henry Thompson, and Burdon Sanderson; history by Edward Dicey, Froude, Sir Henry Maine, Max Müller, Sir Henry Rawlinson, Dr. Russell, and Professor Seeley; theology by the Bishop of Gloucester, Cardinal Manning, Dean Kitchin, Dr. Martineau, Archdeacon Farrar, Dean

Vaughan, and the Rev. Henry White; the Army by Lord Wolseley, Sir Charles Warren, and Sir Charles Wilson; fiction by William Black, R.D. Blackmore, Wilkie Collins, Charles Reade, Charlotte Yonge; dramatic literature by Hermann Merivale, John Hollingshead, and Moy Thomas; journalism by George Augustus Sala; in fact, everything was represented.

In the first year of our existence, again, another very curious and unexpected piece of good fortune happened to us: Sir Robert Fowler, then Lord Mayor of London, invited the Society, as a Society, to a banquet at the Mansion House. The importance to us, at that moment, of such public recognition cannot be exaggerated. We were suddenly, and unexpectedly, dragged out into the light and exhibited to the world. And what with newspaper controversies, publications, public meetings, and public dinners, we have been very much before the world ever since. But our first public recognition we owe to Sir Robert Fowler.

As yet, however, we were an army of officers without any rank and file. We had to enlist recruits. It has been our object ever since, not so much to persuade people that we are proposing and actually doing good work, as to persuade them that it is the bounden duty of everyone engaged in the literary calling to support the only association which exists in this country for the maintenance and definition of their property. The slow growth of the Society, in spite of all the encouragement we received, shows the difficulties we had in this direction. Take the figures from the annual reports. In the first year, 1884, there were only 68 paying members; in 1886 there were only 153—and that in the third year of our existence; in 1888 there were 240; in 1889, 372; in 1891, 662; and in 1892, this year, up to the present day, there have been 870, which of course does not include 25 who have paid up life membership, 20 honorary members, and 50 who may or may not pay, and if they do not, will cease to be members. So slowly have we grown; so difficult has it been to persuade those who actually benefit by our labours openly to join our company.

We met at first in Mr. Scoones's chambers. Garrick Street. After a few months we met in the offices of our first secretary and solicitor, Mr. Tristram Valentine. Then we took a step in advance, and engaged a modest office of our own. It was on the second floor of a house in Cecil Street, over the office of an income tax collector, who never asked us for anything. We had—when we took that step—really no more than one hundred members; some of us had to become life members in order to find the preliminary expenses. How modest that office was! How simple was its furniture! Yet it is never unpleasant for a self-made man to look back at the beginnings, or for the self-made society—which we certainly are—to consider the day of small things.

This was in February 1885, after more than a year of existence. We were still floundering; we were still in uncertainty; we had not yet found out even the first step in the right direction. Most fortunately we were prudent enough not to commit any extravagances. We were restrained from follies, I think, by the lawyers who were on our committee. Happily, we brought forward no charges, denounced no persons, and condemned no systems. We kept very quiet, considering the situation, making investigations and acquiring knowledge. Nothing, I now perceive, more clearly proves the general discontent among men and women of letters than the fact that, though we did nothing all this time—or next to nothing—our numbers, as you have seen, steadily, though slowly, increased. We had now, however, obtained the services—the gratuitous services—of a gentleman whose name must always be remembered in connection with our early history—Mr. Alexander Gait Ross, who became our honorary secretary.

At this time I, who had been preliminary chairman during the first organisation of the Society, retired, and the late Mr. Cotter Morison was elected chairman. Let me take this opportunity of acknowledging the resolution, the wisdom, and the moderation with which Mr. Cotter Morison filled that post. The mere fact that a man of his great personal character was our chairman greatly increased the confidence of the public. He resigned the post a year or two later, when he was attacked by the disease which killed him. Great as was the loss to literature by his death, it was a blow to ourselves from which it seems to me that we have never wholly recovered. Even now, in all times of difficulty, I instinctively feel that if Cotter Morison were only with us, the difficulty would be far more easily faced, and far more wisely surmounted. The place of Mr. Cotter Morison was taken by the late Sir Frederick Pollock, who, from the very beginning, had shown a keen interest in the prospect and progress of the Society. His tenure of office was short, and not marked by anything more than the steady advance of our objects. On his retirement, owing also to ill-health, the committee did me the honour of electing me to take the post.

Now, when it became gradually known that such a society as this existed, that a secretary was in the office all day long, and that he held consultations for nothing with all comers, all those who were in trouble over their books, all those who had grievances and quarrels, began to come to us for advice and assistance. In this way began that part of the Society's work which is generally understood by the world; and in this way began our early troubles. Because, you see, it was a very easy thing to hear and to receive a case; the difficulty was how to find a remedy or to obtain justice where the case demanded either. We did sometimes find a remedy, and we did obtain justice in many cases. But partly from want of funds, and partly from the unwillingness of victims to take action, several cases fell to the ground.

After a little time we abandoned our first organisation of vice-presidents and committee, and substituted a council. We also incorporated ourselves into a company. We had the good fortune to secure the services of Mr. Underdovvn, Q.C., as our honorary counsel, and of Messrs. Field, Roscoe & Co. as our solicitors. Turning back to our first circular, and to the three divisions of work laid down, let us take the international copyright clause first. At the stage at which the American Bill had then arrived, very little could be done, except, as our American friends strongly recommended, to stop as much as lay in our power the calling of names. We had, in fact, as was pointed out by Mr. Brander Matthews and other Americans, been doing on this side exactly what the Americans were doing on their side—pirating books. It was absurd to keep calling the Americans thieves and pirates while our people did exactly the same thing on a smaller scale. It exasperated Americans and weakened the efforts of those who were manfully fighting in the cause of international honesty. Such influence as we possessed we brought to bear in this direction, with, one hopes and believes, a certain allaying of irritation.*

As regards the consolidation of the copyright laws, our action has been more direct and far more important. In fact, there are some who think that our action under this head is more important to the cause of literature than anything else that we have achieved or attempted, for in this direction there was no hesitation or any doubt as to what was wanted. Things chaotic had to be reduced to order, and only a new Act could do it. We appointed a copyright committee, consisting of Sir Frederick Pollock, Mr. Lely, Mr. Fraser Rae, Mr. Ross, and

---

* The United States of America granted copyright under certain conditions to British authors in 1891. This measure, though enacted at the date upon which Sir Walter Besant was writing, had not yet produced practical effect.

Mr. W. Oliver Hodges as honorary secretary, and with the assistance of Mr. Underdown, our honorary counsel, and Mr. Rolt, of the Inner Temple, a new Copyright Bill was drafted. This Bill was submitted to the London Chamber of Commerce for their consideration, and adopted by that body. It was then introduced into the House of Lords by Lord Monkswell, and read a first time. It will be a great thing in the history of the Society to record that it has actually accomplished the consolidation of the various Copyright Acts into one working and intelligible Act.*

Now all this time we were receiving continually accounts, agreements, letters, and cases. The daily correspondence had become very heavy. We therefore gave Mr. Ross a coadjutor in Mr. James Stanley Little, who was our secretary for two years. He retired owing to pressure of his own literary work, and was succeeded by Mr. S. Squire Sprigge, who remained with us for four years, until our work became too much for him, taken with his other engagements. He therefore left us, but remains on our committee. One must not omit to acknowledge that during his four years of office he was the spring and soul of the society, and that our rapid advance during that time is mainly owing to his energies. He was succeeded by Mr. G. Herbert Thring.

Meantime we had been slowly arriving at the comprehension of the fact that, in order to defend literary property, we must understand exactly what it is, of what extent, how it is created, how it is administered, how it should be safeguarded. The first step in advance was when, at a public meeting, held at Willis's Rooms, we laid down the sound principle that publishers' accounts, like those of any other enterprise in which two or more persons are jointly interested, must be subject to audit, as a simple right and a simple precaution. This right was publicly acknowledged by Messrs. Longman & Co., who were followed by other publishers, but not by all. Since then we have devoted a great deal of attention to ascertaining exactly what the copyright of a book and its publication may mean as actual property. There has been a stream of abuse, detraction, and wilful misrepresentation of our work poured

* The Bill was read a second time in the House of Lords about ten years ago; and though it was not proceeded with further, it became the starting-point for future effort. In 1896 a non-contentious amending Bill was drafted by the Society of Authors, and read in the House of Lords, and in 1898 Lord Thring consented to draft a Bill dealing with literary, dramatic, and musical copyright. This Bill will probably form the basis of future legislation.

upon us continually. Chiefly, we have been reviled for daring to ask what our own property means. This abuse shows, first, the hostility of those who desire to conceal and hush up the truth as regards the buying and selling of books. That is a matter of course; such hostility was to be expected, and, with all the misrepresentations that can be devised and invented, must be taken as part of the day's work. It has been, as you perhaps know, a good part of my day's work, during the last five years, to silence this opposition. I am happy to think that every such misrepresentation published in a newspaper or in a magazine has only resulted in an accession of new members and in an increase in public confidence. But, in addition to the opposition of interested persons, we have had to encounter a very unexpected and remarkable opposition from those who ought to be our own friends—certain authors and certain journalists. Into the history and motives and reason of this opposition I should like with your permission to inquire.

There has existed for a hundred and fifty years at least, and there still lingers among us, a feeling that it is unworthy the dignity of letters to take any account at all of the commercial or pecuniary side. No one, you will please to remark, has ever thought of reproaching the barrister, the solicitor, the physician, the surgeon, the painter, the sculptor, the actor, the singer, the musician, the architect, the chemist, the engineer, the clergyman, or any other kind of brain worker that one can mention, with taking fees or salaries or money for his work; nor does anyone reproach these men with looking after their fees and getting rich it they can. Nor does anyone suggest that to consider the subject of payment very carefully—to take ordinary precautions against dishonesty—brings discredit on anyone who does so; nor does anyone call that barrister unworthy of the Bar who expects large fees in proportion to his name and his ability; nor does anyone call that painter a tradesman whose price advances with his reputation. I beg you to consider this point very carefully, for the moment any author begins to make practical investigation into the value—the monetary value—of the work which he puts upon the market, a hundred voices arise from those of his own craft as well as from those who live by administering his property— voices which cry out upon the sordidness, the meanness, the degradation of turning literature into a trade. We hear, I say, this kind of talk from our own ranks—though, one must own, chiefly from those who never had an opportunity of discovering what literary property means. Does, I ask, this cry mean anything at all? Well, first of all, it manifestly means a confusion of ideas. There are two values of literary work—distinct, separate, not commensurable—they cannot be measured, they cannot be considered together. The one is the literary value of a work—its artistic, poetic, dramatic value, its value of accuracy, of construction, of presentation, of novelty, of style, of magnetism. On that value is based the real position of every writer in his own generation, and the estimate of him, should he survive, for generations to follow. I do not greatly blame those who cry out upon the connection of literature with trade: they are jealous, and rightly jealous, for the honour of letters. We will acknowledge so much. But the confusion lies in not understanding that every man who takes money for whatever he makes or does may be regarded, in a way, and not offensively, as a tradesman, but that the making of a thing need have nothing whatever to do with the price it will command; and that this price in the case of a book cannot be measured by the literary or artistic value.

In other words, while an artist is at work upon a poem, a drama, or a romance, this aspect of his work, and this alone, is in his mind, otherwise his work would be naught. But once finished and ready for production, then comes in the other value—the commercial value, which is a distinct thing. Here the artist ceases and the man of business begins. Either the man of business begins at this point or the next steps of that artist infallibly bring him to disaster, or at least the partial loss of that commercial value. Remember that any man who has to sell a thing must make himself acquainted with its value, or he will be— what? Call it what you please—over-reached, deluded, cheated. That is a recognised rule in every other kind of business. Let us do our best to make it recognised in our own.

Apart from this confusion of ideas between literary and commercial value, there is another and a secondary reason for this feeling. For two hundred years, at least, contempt of every kind has been poured upon the literary hack, who is, poor wretch, the unsuccessful author. Why? We do not pour contempt upon the unsuccessful painter who has to make the pot boil with pictures at 15s. each. Clive Newcome came down to that, and a very pitiful, tearful scene in the story it is—full of pity and of tears. If he had been a literary hack, where would have been the pity and the tears? In my experience at the Society, I have come across many most pitiful cases, where the man who has failed is doomed to lead a life which is one long tragedy of grinding, miserable, underpaid work, with no hope and no relief possible—one long tragedy of endurance

WALTER BESANT

and hardship. I am not accusing anyone; I call no names; very likely such a man gets all he deserves; his are the poor wages of incompetence; his is the servitude of the lowest work; his is the contumely of hopeless poverty; his is the derision of the critic. But we laugh at such a wretch, and call him a literary hack. Why, I ask, when we pity the unsuccessful in every other line, do we laugh at and despise the unsuccessful author?

Once more, this contempt—real or pretended—for money, what does it mean? Sir Walter Scott did not despise the income which he made by his books, nor did Byron, nor did Dickens, Thackeray, George Eliot, Charles Reade, Wilkie Collins, Macaulay, nor, in fact, any single man or woman in the history of letters who has ever succeeded. This pretended contempt, then—does it belong to those who have not succeeded? It is sometimes assumed by them; more often one finds it in articles written for certain papers by sentimental ladies who are not authors. Wherever it is found, it is always lingering somewhere; always we come upon this feeling—ridiculous, senseless, and baseless—that it is beneath the dignity of an author to manage his business matters as a man of business should, with the same regard for equity in his agreement, the same resolution to know what is meant by both sides of an agreement, and the same jealousy as to assigning the administration of his property.

Again, how did the contempt rise? It came to us as a heritage of the last century. In the course of our investigations into the history of literary property—the result of which will, I hope, appear some day in a volume form—I recently caused a research to be made into the business side of literature in the last century. Publishers were not then men of education and knowledge, as many of them are at the present moment; they were not advised by scholars, men of taste and intuition; the market, compared with that of the present day, was inconceivably small; there were great risks, due to all these causes. The practice, therefore, was, in view of these risks, to pay the author so much for his book right out, and to expect a successful book to balance, and more than balance, one that was unsuccessful. Therefore they bought the books they published at the lowest price they could persuade the author to accept. Therefore—the consequence follows like the next line in Euclid—the author began to appear to the popular imagination as a suppliant standing hat in hand beseeching the generosity of the bookseller. Physician and barrister stood upright, taking the recognised fee. The author bent a humble back, holding his hat in one humble hand, while he held out the other humble hand for as many guineas as he could get. That, I say, was the popular view of the author. And it still lingers among us. There are, in other callings, if we think of it, other professional contempts. Everybody acknowledges that teaching is a noble work, but everybody formerly despised the schoolmaster because he was always flogging boys—no imagination can regard with honour and envy the man who is all day long caning and flogging. The law is a noble study, but everybody formerly despised the attorney, with whom the barrister would neither shake hands nor sit at table. Medicine is a noble study, but the surgeon was formerly despised because in bygone days he was closely connected with the barber. Do not let us be surprised, therefore, if the author, who had to take whatever was given to him, came to be regarded as a poor helpless suppliant.

The kind of language even now sometimes used illustrates a lingering of the old feeling. We constantly read here and there of the generosity of a publisher. My friends, let us henceforth resolve to proclaim that we do not want generosity; that we will not have it; that we are not beggars and suppliants, and that what we want is the administration of our own property—or its purchase—on fair, just, and honourable terms. Let us remember that the so-called generosity must be either a dole— an alms—over and above his just claim, in which case it degrades the author to take it, and robs the publisher who gives it; or it is a payment under the just value, when it degrades the publisher who gives it, while it robs the author who takes it.

I return to the history of the Society. When our office was discovered, so to speak, by the outside world, I have said that there began to be poured in upon us a continuous stream, which has never ceased, of agreements, accounts, proposals, estimates, and letters between publishers and authors. From the examination and the comparison of these documents, from other matter obtained of printers, from communications made to us by persons formerly engaged in publishing offices, and from every possible source of information, we arrived at a knowledge of the business side of literature which is certainly unrivalled by that possessed by any man, even by any man actually engaged in publishing. We know especially by experience that a system which demands blind confidence on one side not only invites a betrayal of that confidence, but must inevitably lead to such a betrayal. There is no body of men in the world who can be trusted not to cheat should a man say to them, "Take my property. Do what you please with it. Bring me what you like for my share. I shall never inquire into your statements or audit your accounts." This is what has been done, and is still done everyday. That man invites fraud who says beforehand that he will not question or doubt the returns.

This being so, we were not at all surprised to find that frauds were being carried on very extensively. Not universally. We have always most carefully made that necessary reservation. We have been constantly accused of charging all publishers as a body with dishonesty. I say again, that five or six years ago, when we had acquired some knowledge of what was going on, we found—with this reservation always carefully insisted upon—a wide spread practice of fraudulent accounts. Is it necessary to enumerate the methods pursued, which were as various as the tricks of the conjurer? There was the overcharge of the cost of production—very common indeed; there was the charge for advertisements which never appeared, or were exchanged and never paid for—also very common; there was the insertion of an enormous estimate of cost of production in the agreement, which the author, after he had signed, could not set aside; there were clauses in the agreement so worded and so mixed up that the author did not know what he gave away; there were charges for things that ought not to be charged—publisher's reader, publisher's lists, publisher's travellers, all kinds of things; there was the royalty so designed as to give three times and four times—any number of times— to the publisher that it gave to the author; there was the purchase of a valuable work for next to nothing. One could find instances by the dozen on looking into the Society's case books, but very considerable improvement has taken place of late in respect to these methods, solely in consequence of the action of the Society.

Without going into court more than once or twice (though in a great many instances an action has been proposed as an alternative) we have succeeded not only in procuring substantial justice in many cases for our clients, but we have also done a great deal to put a stop to the former prevalent abuses. A point in our favour has been the extreme moderation of our demands. We have claimed, in fact, so far, only three points: (1) That we must have the right of audit; (2) that in any agreement based on royalties we must know what the agreement gives to either side; and (3) that there must be no secret profits. We prepared and published a book, the like of which, it is certain, has never before appeared in any country. It was called the *Methods of Publishing*. In this book a specimen of every known form of publishing was taken from agreements and accounts actually in our possession. Nothing was invented; they were actual real agreements that were quoted. With each agreement the meaning of the various clauses was explained. It is a book of the greatest value to everyone who wants to know how to conduct his own business for himself, and desires to avoid pitfalls and traps and the many dangers pointed out. This book, however, useful as it was, proved to be insufficient. There was still wanting something to supplement the information contained in it. By the comparison of any agreement submitted to an author with the corresponding agreement contained in this book, he might come to a pretty safe conclusion as to the value or fairness of his own. But he wanted more; he wanted to know, as nearly as possible, the cost of producing his own book, the manner in which it was placed upon the market, and the results under certain given conditions. That information we found for him. It cost us a very great deal of patience and of time. You can hardly understand the trouble it was to get at the figures; at last they were obtained and passed by three—or perhaps four—firms of responsible printers. Of course, we do not say that we have found the exact cost, because there is no such thing. A printer's bill is elastic, and varies from firm to firm, and time to time; but the figures are, if anything, above the mark, and some accounts have been sent in to us where the details were below our figures.

By the publication of this book, called the *Cost of Production*, together with that called the *Methods of Publication*, we have, I submit, rendered a very signal service to the independence of the author. He now understands what kind of property he holds in his MS. He can say, "Should this work prove successful—commercially successful—it will produce so much for the first thousand, so much for the second, and so on. What share does the publisher claim for the distribution, collection, and administration of this work?" At all events, if circumstances oblige him to take what is unfair, he will know it; he will speak of it—the thing will become noised abroad, the reputation of that publisher will suffer. What we have done is to throw light—always more and more light—into every part and every detail of our own business. We have enabled authors, in a word, to meet men of business as men of business.

I hasten to complete this history by the brief record of the points of less importance. We have ascertained, by an inquiry conducted for us in the most important colonies, that there was, before the passing of the American Copyright Act, a considerable trade in pirated books. We have called the attention of the Minister for the Colonies to this trade, and steps have been taken to stop the piracy. We have investigated and published an account of the administration of the Civil List from its beginning. We have founded for our own purposes a paper which is devoted entirely to the accumulation of facts and the dissemination of teaching in our own business relations.

Our office has become the recognised refuge for all who are in trouble or doubt. People come to us for advice on all subjects connected with literary property. The cases always in the secretary's hands average at any moment about a dozen. As fast as one is cleared off, another one comes in. The correspondence increases daily; from all parts of the country and from the colonies the letters pour in.

We have been accused of fostering the ambitions of the incapable, and of helping to flood the market with trash. Far from it; we dissuade by every means in our power the incapable; we have readers who give them the plain truth; we advertise warnings against paying for the publication of MSS. But I confess that we can do little to keep down the swelling stream of aspirants. Thousands of pens are flying over the paper at this moment and every moment, producing bad novels and worse poetry. We check some of them; the rest must learn by bitter disappointment. Do not, however, let us talk about flooding the market; that is a mere conventional phrase. Thousands of bad books may be produced, but they never get circulated; nobody buys them; they drop still-born from the press; they swell the statistics alone.

To sum up, we have taken steps to reduce our copyright law from chaos to order; we have investigated and made public the various methods of publishing, and have shown what each means; we have placed in the hands of every author the means of ascertaining for himself what his property may mean; we have examined and exposed the facts connected with the Civil Pension List. What do we intend to do in the future? Here I must speak for myself. First, I look for the enlargement of the Society to four times, ten times, its present numbers. Everyone who writes—the journalists who lead the thought of the world, the teachers of all kinds, the scientific men,the medical men, the theologians, the creators in imaginative work—everyone who writes a single book should consider it his duty to belong to us. With this extension of our numbers we shall create funds for special purposes, for fighting actions if necessary. There are certain disputed points which can only be settled in the courts. We shall give our journal wider aims.

I should very much like to see established an institute akin to the Law Institute, but what I want, even more than the institute, is a Pension

Fund. That, I see plainly, is above all to be desired. I want a Pension Fund such as that which the Société des Gens de Lettres in Paris has established, where everyone in his turn receives a pension, and it is not a dole or a charity, but a right. The member is not obliged to take that pension; if he chooses, he can refuse it; then it goes to swell the pensions of those who want the assistance. We have been too much occupied during these last years for this fund to be so much as started. Perhaps, however, the committee may see their way at no distant period to attempt the thing. A Pension Fund is absolutely necessary for the completion of the independence of literature.*

There were many other societies in which I was interested. Those which were strictly philanthropic I reserve for another chapter. I was initiated into freemasonry as far back as 1862. On my return to England I joined a lodge. I have never been an enthusiast for the rites and ceremonies of the craft, but I have always understood its great capabilities as a social and religious force. Properly carried out, the freemason has friends everywhere, and in case of need, brethren of the same fraternity are bound by vow to assist him. Every lodge is a benefit club; the members are bound to each other by the vows and obligations of a mediæval guild. The craft has developed a species of doctrine, vague and without a defined creed, which is to some of its members a veritable religion. It is, above all, a religion which requires no priest, no Church standing between man and his Creator; it does not recognise any superstitious or supernatural claims. It is therefore a bulwark against the Roman Catholic religion or any Romanising practices; and, as such, is very properly excommunicated by the Roman Catholic Church.

The origins of Masonry are imperfectly understood. This I had always felt to be a serious defect, although, the craft being what it is acknowledged to be, the origin is not an essential point. However, there was existing a small—a very small—society called the Masonic Archaeological Institute. Of this I became the honorary secretary. We had papers read; some of them were useful, some were rubbish; after a while I handed over the papers and my office to Mr. Haliburton, of Nova Scotia, who was then living in London, and I heard no more about the institute, which died a natural death. But some eighteen years later there was established an archaeological lodge consisting of nine persons,

---

* The Pension Fund of the Society of Authors has since been started.

WALTER BESANT

of whom I was one. It was proposed to carry this on as a medium for historical papers on all points connected with the craft. The secretary, one of the nine, has developed this lodge until it has, besides its original members, some two thousand corresponding members scattered about the whole world. Once at Albany, New York, I received a visit from one of the corresponding members, who got together a few Freemasons of that city to give me a welcome. The thing was a trifle; but it made me realise the great success and the widespread influence of the Lodge "Quatuor Coronati."

One more society. In 1879 or 1880 a little company of a dozen or so met at a certain tavern and dined together, the dinner being the foundation of the Rabelais Club. This for eight years or so was a highly flourishing club. We dined together about six times a year; we had no speeches and but one toast—"The Master." We mustered some seventy or eighty members, and we used to lay on the table leaflets, verses, and all kinds of literary triflings. These were afterwards collected and formed three volumes called *Recreations of the Rabelais Club,* only a hundred copies of each being printed. Among the members were Edwin Abbey, R.C. Christie (author of the life of Etienne Dolet), George Du Maurier, Thomas Hardy, Bret Harte, Colonel John Hay, Oliver Wendell Holmes, Henry Irving, Henry James, C.G. Leland, Earl Lytton, Lord Houghton, James Payn, J.E. Millais, Professor Palmer, Sir Frederick Pollock, Walter Pollock, Saintsbury, Sala, W.F. Smith (latest and best translator of Rabelais), R. Louis Stevenson, Alma-Tadema, Toole, Herbert Stephen, H.D. Traill, and Woolner.

The *Recreations* contain a good deal that is indifferent and a good deal that is good. Among the latter is some truly excellent fooling by Sir Frederick Pollock; there are verses by Du Maurier; there are verses by Professor Palmer—notably a short collection called "Arabesques from the Bazaars," supposed to be narrated by one Colonel Abdullah. Of these I quote one called:—

THE STORY OF THE ASTROLOGER.

"Alack a day, for the days of old
When heads were clever and hearts were true,
And a Caliph scattered stores of gold
On men, my Ali, like me and you

"Haroun was moody, Haroun was sad,
 And he drank a glass of wine or two;
 But it only seemed to make him mad,
 And the cup at the Sakis' head he threw.

"Came Yahya* in; and he dodged the glass
 That all too near his turban flew;
 And he bowed his head, and he said, 'Alas!
 Your Majesty seems in a pretty stew!'

"'And well I may,' the monarch said;
 'And so, my worthy friend, would you,
 If you knew that you must needs be dead
 And buried, perhaps, in a day or two.'

"'For the man who writes the almanacks—
 Ez Zadkiel, a learned Jew—
 Has found, amongst other distressing facts,
 That the days I have left upon earth are few.'

"'Call up the villain!' the vizier cried,
 'That he may have the reward that's due,
 For having, the infidel, prophesied
 A thing that is plainly quite untrue.'

"The Caliph waved his hand, and soon
 A dozen dusky eunuchs flew;
 And back in a trice before Haroun
 They set the horoscopic Jew.

"'Now tell me, sirrah!' says Yahya, 'since
 From astral knowledge so well you knew
 The term of the life of our sovereign prince,
 How many years are left to you?'

---

* Yahya the Barmecide was Haroun al Raschid's Prime Minister. He was the father of
Jaafer, whose incognito walks through Bagdad are a favourite theme in *The Arabian Nights*.

WALTER BESANT

> *"May Allah lengthen the vizier's days!*
> *His Highness' loss all men would rue;*
> *Some eighty years, my planet says,*
> *Is the number that I shall reach unto.'*

> *"A single stroke of Yahya's sword*
> *Has severed the Jew's neck quite clean through—*
> *'Now tell me, sire, if the fellow's word*
> *Seems, after that, in the least bit true?'*

> *"Haroun he smiled, and a purse of gold*
> *He handed over to Yahya true;*
> *And the heedless corpse, all white and cold,*
> *The eunuchs in the gutter threw.*

> *"What loyalty that act displays,*
> *Combined with a sense of humour too—*
> *Ah, Ali! those were palmy days!*
> *And those Barmecides, what a lot they knew!"*

In 1889 the Rabelais Club fell to pieces. Perhaps we had gone on long enough; perhaps we spoiled the club by admitting visitors. However, the club languished and died.

XIII

Philanthropic Work

I t is instructive to consider how I dropped without any effort on my own part, even unconsciously, into philanthropic work and effort.

It all began with a novel. In 1880 and in 1881 I spent a great deal of time walking about the mean monotony of the East End of London. It was not a new field to me. That is to say, I had already seen some of it— the river-side. Hackney, Whitechapel, and Bethnal Green; but I had never before realised the vast extent of the eastern city, its wonderful collection of human creatures; its possibilities; the romance that lies beneath its monotony; the tragedies and the comedies, the dramas that are always playing themselves out in this huge hive of working bees.

Gradually, out of the whole, as sometimes happens when the gods are favourable, a few figures detached themselves from the crowd and stood before me to be drawn. And presently I understood that one of the things very much wanted in this great place was a centre of organised recreation, orderly amusement, and intellectual and artistic culture. So I pictured an heiress going down to the place under the disguise of a dressmaker, and I showed how little by little the same idea was forced upon her; how she was aided in this discovery by a young man who by birth, not by education, belonged to the place; and how in obedience to their invitation the Palace of Delight arose. The rest has been told a hundred times. Sir Edmund Currie, trying to create such a place, used the book as a text-book. The Palace was built. It was opened in 1887.

I have often been asked what the Palace has done. It has done a great deal; but it has not done one-quarter, not one-tenth part, of what it might have done. It was built and furnished with a noble hall, a swimming bath, a splendid organ, a complete gymnasium, one of the finest library buildings in London, a winter garden, art schools, and a lecture room. Unfortunately a polytechnic was tacked on to it; the original idea of a place of recreation was mixed up with a place of education.

More money was wanted. I hoped that Sir Edmund, who was greatly respected in the City, would, as he half promised, boom it in the City. But he did not. However, we started with all the things mentioned above, and with billiard-rooms, with a girls' social side, with a debating society, with clubs for all kinds of things—cricket, football, rambles, and the like; we had delightful balls in the great hall, we had concerts and organ recitals, the girls gave dances in their social rooms; there was a literary society; we had lectures and entertainments, orchestral performances and part singing; nothing could have been better than our start. We had a library committee, of which I was the chairman. We collected together about fifteen thousand volumes—that is to say, we made a most excellent beginning. Everything did not go on quite well. At the billiard tables, which were very popular, the young men took to betting, and it was thought best to stop billiards altogether. The literary club proved a dead failure; not a soul, while I was connected with the Palace, showed the least literary ability or ambition. Still the successes far outweighed the failures.

Then we heard that the Drapers' Company proposed to take over the Palace and to run it at their own cost and expense. I have no wish to appear to be bringing charges against the Drapers' Company. Let me, however, instance their treatment of the library. We gave them, as I said, fifteen thousand volumes in good condition. We had three ladies as librarians—most efficient librarians they were. They ruled over the rough people who came to the library with a gentle but a steady hand. There was no such thing as a row while they were there. Now, such a library costs, in the maintenance of the fabric, in the binding and preservation of the books, in salaries, wages, lights, cleaning, newspapers and magazines, from £1,000 to £1,200 a year. The Company took over the Palace on an understanding that it should be kept up. The library was an integral part of the Palace. What have they done? They have dismissed the librarians, they have refused the money necessary for binding and preserving the books, they have bought no new books and have made no appeal for any, they have appointed no library committee, they have reduced the staff to a man and a boy. All those books out of our fifteen thousand which are in demand are dropping to pieces; and the Company are trying to hand over the lovely building, which is, I say, an integral part of the Palace, to the poverty-stricken ratepayers of the parish. So much for the library.

As regards the recreative side, the Company cannot put down the concerts; but they have stopped the baths, they have closed the winter gardens, they have stopped the girls' social side; they have turned the place into a polytechnic and nothing else—except for one or two things which they cannot prevent.

However, the Palace has raised the standard of music enormously; the people know and appreciate good music. They have had some good exhibitions of pictures and of industries; and there is an excellent polytechnic in the building. But alas! alas! what might not the Palace have done for the people if the original design had been carried out, if no educational side had been attached, and if the Drapers' Company had never touched it?

Three years after the appearance of the novel in which the Palace of Delight was described, I wrote another touching a note of deeper resonance. This book was the most truthful of anything that I have ever written. It was called *Children of Gibeon*. It offered the daily life and the manners—so far as they can be offered without offensive and useless realism—of the girls who do the rougher and coarser work of sewing in their own lodgings. I say that this book was as truthful as a long and patient investigation could make it. I knew every street in Hoxton; I knew also every street in Ratcliffe; I had been about among the people day after day and week after week—neglecting almost everything else. The thing was absorbing. I had stood in the miserable back room where the woman living by herself—the grey-haired elderly woman, all alone in that awful cell, with no furniture but sacking on the floor—is stitching away for bare life. I had sat among the girls whom I described—three in a room, with the one broad bed for the three—also stitching away for bare life. I had seen the widow and the daughter hot-pressing, stitching, their fingers flying for bare life. All these things and people I saw over and over again till my heart was sore and my brain was weary with the contemplation of so much misery. And then I sat down to write. Did the book do any good? I do not know. I heard among the Hoxton folk that certain firms which had been in the habit of fining their girls for small offences were ashamed to own that this was their practice, and refrained. So far it was useful in abolishing a cruel and tyrannical act of oppression. What else it did I know not. Perhaps it made employers more careful in their treatment of the girls, more considerate, kinder in speech and manner. That it ran up wages I cannot believe, because sentiment has nothing to do with wages.

The book, however, introduced me to certain clubs of working girls. These clubs, run by ladies, are carrying on a noble work. Unfortunately there are not enough of them, and they reach comparatively few of the class for whom they are designed. They exact from the ladies who

WALTER BESANT

conduct them the sacrifice of all their evenings—often of all their lives. It is a great deal to ask of ladies. On the other hand they have their reward in the salvation and the rescue of the girls. It is difficult to think of any sacrifice which a woman can make, that is more entirely lovely and more truly Christian, than to undertake the management of such a girls' club. What is the life of a nun, what the life of a sister immured in a cloister, compared with the life of a woman whose work and wage are wholly given to her sister, the girl who makes the buttonhole at the starvation wage of elevenpence-halfpenny a gross?

There followed on the *Children of Gibeon* an attempt at organising co-operation for working women. The attempt was made by Mrs. Heckford, who, with her husband, founded the Children's Hospital at Poplar. She started with a small house in or near Cable Street, and with a dozen girls. She began very well. They made shirts, they obeyed the directress, there was a forewoman in whom Mrs. Heckford placed unbounded trust. One day she found that this forewoman had betrayed her confidence; she had gone off, taking with her half the girls, in order to start on her own account a sweating establishment. By what persuasions she induced the girls to leave a place where they were treated with the greatest kindness and personal affection and were earning half as much again as in a sweater's den, I know not. Fear of giving offence, and of being refused work by the sweater, if they should be thrown out of work, was probably the leading motive. However, half the girls went away. Then Mrs. Heckford took a larger house and made a bid for different kinds of business. Well, the attempt failed; the women were not educated to co-operation; sweating they understood. They would like themselves to become sweaters if they could; the sweater, remember, is as a rule only one degree better off than the women sweated, very nearly as poor, very nearly as miserable; but he, or she, represents the first upward step. From being a sweater to the trade, one may become a master of sweaters.

The next step, so far as I remember, was the foundation of a committee to consider the whole question of working women and their pay. We went, we talked; certain persons gave us small sums, which we spent in accumulating facts and evidence. This evidence we printed. Then we discovered that Mr. Charles Booth was doing on a large and fully organised scale what we were attempting on a small and limited scale. I have now, somewhere, the bundle of printed tables which represent our work. But the committee's work came to nothing more.

Meantime, as was inevitable, considering that I had so many things to do, I lost touch with Hoxton and Stepney. I dropped out of the governing body of the People's Palace. In fact, they did not re-elect me; I suppose because I so seldom attended the meetings, at which the Drapers' Company more and more carried matters their own way—which was not the way for which the Palace was designed. There was, however, one place in which I continued to take a personal interest. It was the parish of St. James's, Ratcliffe, then under the charge of the Rev. R.K. Arbuthnot. It is certainly one of the poorest parishes in all London. It consisted, until a few streets were pulled down, of about eight thousand people. Of these, three-fourths were Roman Catholics and Irish, but there was no division among the people on account of religion. The parish contained a church, a "mission church" under the arches, schools, a "doss-house" for the destitute, a Quakers' meeting-house on the edge of the boundary—perhaps, indeed, belonging to another parish. There were in the parish no professional men, no doctor even; no Roman Catholic chapel; and in not a single house except those of the clergy was there a servant. The parish was "run" by the clergy, and by the ladies who lived in, and worked for, the place, giving all their work, all their thoughts, and all their lives to the people. They had a girls' club numbering from forty to fifty. The girls came to the club every night; they talked, they sang, they danced, they learned needlework, they were on terms of friendliness and personal affection with the leaders; every night they had three hours' quiet, learning unconsciously lessons of self-respect and order. At ten, or thereabouts, when prayers began, they all got up and stepped out—quietly, not to give offence; and went back to Brook Street, their boulevard, where they met their young men, and walked about arm in arm working off some of their animal spirits.

The ladies at one time had also a lads' club; it was carried on by one lady who had an extraordinary power of influencing these lads. They were fellows of fourteen to eighteen, great hulking fellows. They mostly worked at odd jobs along the river-side; they were full of boisterous spirits and ready at any moment to make hay of everything in the club. But they did not; the slim delicate girl restrained them. She made them put on the gloves with each other, and that shook the devil out of them for the evening; then she read to them, told them stories, made them play at games, and persuaded them to be content and happy in the quiet room with warmth and light. The place was the rickety old warehouse which had been Mrs. Heckford's first Children's Hospital. But the place was condemned—not before it was time; the flooring had become rotten, the whole house threatened to come down. The boys were turned out, and the house is now, I believe, with the whole street of crazy warehouses and tumble-down cottages, undermined.

At the same time another club held in the same place was destroyed. This was the children's playhouse. The principal room of the house— that on the ground floor—had been taken over by the same lady for the little children. When they came out of school at four o'clock, there was nowhere for them to go. Therefore, in the cold and dark winter evenings, in the rain and snow and frost, these little mites played about in the street and on the kerb. Then the room was given to them, with its blazing fire and its gas; a small collection of toys was made for them, chiefly of the india rubber kind, which they could not break; and from half-past four till half-past seven they would play about in this room under shelter and protected from the cold. The directress was with them most of the time; she concluded every evening with a little service held in an upstairs room, which she had fitted as a chapel. One of her rough lads, who would otherwise have been a "hooligan," played the harmonium for them; they sang a hymn—these tender little children—they said a prayer or two on their knees, and so went home. If I could afford it, I would build for the parish a house, with a room where the children could play and sing and pray; and a room where the lads could be taken in hand without fuss or parade and could be reduced to order by the beneficent autocrat who ruled over the lads of Ratcliffe.

Another form of practical philanthropy which was laid upon me, so to speak, was caused not by anything I had written, but by the action of a friend. In the year 1879, my old friend Charles G. Leland (Hans Breitmann), who had been long resident in England and on the Continent, returned to Philadelphia, his native town; and there proceeded to realise a much cherished project of establishing an evening school for the teaching and practice of the minor arts—wood-carving, leather-work, fretwork, work in iron and other metals, cabinet-making, weaving, embroidery, and so forth. The attempt proved to be a very great success; very shortly he found himself with classes containing in the aggregate four hundred pupils. He then proposed to me that we should start a similar school here in England. As he was coming back, I suggested that we should wait until his arrival. We did so, and on his return we started the society called the Home Arts Association. We had as secretary a lady who had been watching the work from the beginning, was familiar with every aspect of it, and understood all its possibilities. I became the treasurer, and we were so fortunate as to interest many influential persons. The idea was taken up by ladies of the highest rank, and by gentlemen with large estates; our schools were started all over the country; we have now, I believe, over five hundred schools; we hold an annual exhibition of work; the demand for articles such as we produce is largely increasing; and we have found evening occupation for hundreds. For my own part, after doing what I could for the Association at the outset, I placed my resignation in the hands of the committee, to be accepted when they chose, because I could do no more for them. Let it be understood, however, that the movement is due entirely to the clear foresight of Charles Leland, and that the success of the English branch is due mainly to the intelligence and the resource of the secretary, Miss Annie Dymes.

A later attempt to improve the position of women was the Women's Bureau of Work. I had long been of opinion that something might and could be done for women by way of creating a central bureau, with offices all over the country and in the colonies, where women who want work, and places which want women workers, might be registered, classified, and made known. Thus I imagined an association which should receive the names of women wanting work as typewriters, translators, shorthand clerks, accountants, teachers, artists, designers, etc., both in London and in the provinces; and would take note also of the wants of workers. The names and the places should be entered in books for every centre, so that a woman in London might hear of work that would suit her at Liverpool and *vice versâ*. The plan had the merit of great simplicity.

After a little private talk on the subject, a meeting was held, Mrs. Creighton being in the chair. I opened the subject by reading a paper; there was a discussion; and in the end the bureau was established. I went to Liverpool and addressed a meeting there on the subject and to Edinburgh and addressed another meeting there. The bureau is now in full working order; I have not heard of late how many local centres are established, but I think that it is only a question of time before a network of branches is spread over the whole country and the colonies. After all the failures and the futile talk about the work of women, it is satisfactory to find that there is something practical and definite actually established for their benefit.

Since then, there are many causes, which seemed to me worthy of support, which I have been invited to assist by speaking or by writing.

The Ragged School Union is one—a most admirable association with a record of unmixed success and practical charity. I wrote a paper on the subject for the *Contemporary Review*. In support of the London Hospital I was invited to write a paper, and did so; it came out in a magazine first, it being understood that I was not to be paid for it, but that I could use it as I chose. I gave it, therefore, to the hospital; they printed it as a pamphlet and circulated it largely, clearing some thousands by the work. They made me in return a governor of the hospital. Concerning the continuation schools, I wrote a paper, also for the *Contemporary*, called "From Fourteen to Seventeen," pointing out the dangers of the streets for the young people after their working hours. The continuation schools have now been established, but those whose zeal outruns their discretion are doing their best to discredit them by claiming, practically, the right to keep open school on all subjects free of charge at the ratepayers' expense—and for the whole wide world. However, good sense will in the end prevail; such a claim reduced to plain English is monstrous.

I have had, besides, to lecture on Art in the Home, on Women's Ideals, on the Science of Recreation, on Free Public Libraries, and on many other topics connected with social life and philanthropic work. I think that I have never written or spoken on any subject which has given me more satisfaction than on the social work of the Salvation Army. It is, indeed, amazing to observe the prejudices against the people of that great Christian community. Huxley called them "corybantic christians." He knew only the external side of their religion, about which I have steadfastly refused to speak. They carry on a religion which wants no priest and has no ecclesiastical pretension. Had Huxley considered this great point, he would perhaps have been a little more tolerant of an aggressiveness which was not directed against himself or his own class. What are the facts? There is a vast company of men and women who carry on the work of a community on the lines laid down for them all over the English-speaking countries. They are called an army in order to secure the discipline and the obedience of an army; they obey orders and are subject to discipline; they are poorly, very poorly, paid; they can make nothing extra for themselves in anyway whatever; they can save nothing; there is no inducement for them to join on account of the pay; the work is incessant, and the harder they work the more are they promoted to still harder work; they have no rewards of fame, or name, or honour, even among themselves; whatever the results of their work, the workers themselves get no reward and no publicity; out of the whole number, not one has a banking account; they live with great plainness in poor quarters—sometimes in rough neighbourhoods, where they are knocked about and ill-treated; they give up whatever luxuries and softness of life they may have known. Sometimes the funds fail; then they go without any money—Heaven knows how—for a week or more. Now all these things they do—for what reason? In the hope of what reward? For the love of God, for the sake of Jesus Christ—and for no other reason whatever. Observe that not even the early followers of Francis lived in greater poverty; not even in the first sprightly running of their pristine zeal, did they endure more, sacrifice more, suffer more, court harder work with greater obscurity.

They carry on, besides their religious propaganda among the poorer classes, a quiet work among the "submerged." They have shelters and night refuges; they receive the prisoners on their release; they bring into their homes both the most miserable, the most abandoned, the most deeply sunken women, and the lads and girls ripening for lives of vice. They have workshops where they train the poor wrecks and the ignorant youths in trades of all kinds; they have labour bureaux, where they find work for those people. As in so many cases a return to the land is the best thing possible, they have a farm where they make of them agricultural labourers, brickmakers, breeders of poultry, horses, and cattle. I repeat that no Franciscan monk in his newborn zeal could excel these so-called captains and lieutenants in the community which calls itself the Salvation Army. I have myself taken their statistics—those which frankly acknowledge their failures—and I have shown that in the farm alone there is room for many more failures, and that an annual gain would still be left. Yet the world refuses to recognise the work; they listen to, and repeat, lies. They allege, falsely, that there is no balance sheet published; they pretend that the chief, General Booth, is enriching himself and his family. Why, no one has a salary more than that which a bank clerk commands after a few years in office; all the money is banked in the General's name, but none can be taken out without the authority of the Finance Committee. In a word, all possible precautions are taken to prevent the things concerning which the dissemination of lies goes on. Yet the lies are disseminated; and they are believed. The reason why they are believed is that the people, seeing an organisation thus successful, outside the ordinary lines, and without the patronage of bishop, clergy, and Church, an organisation which is essentially popular—of the people, for the people, by the people—an organisation containing here and there a scholar and a gentleman and a gentlewoman, but consisting for the most part of a simple folk, regard it with suspicion and are slow to recognise the solid feats of self-sacrifice, the Christian aims—and the success.

The general prejudice against the Salvation Army was illustrated in an article in the *Spectator* in the autumn of 1900. The writer, after speaking of the early Friars, asked sadly where such a spirit of self-sacrifice and devotion was to be found at the present day. The spirit was manifested in a great work—far greater than that of Francis in his lifetime; that work was lying at the very feet of the writer; yet he could not see it; all he saw was an aggressive form of sectarian Christianity. Here is the vast machinery worked by thousands for the sake of tens of thousands, bringing hope and consolation and the restoration of manhood to the poor wrecks and waifs of humanity, to the submerged, to the criminals, to the drunkards, to the prostitutes, to the discharged prisoners, to ruined clerks, to broken gentlemen. "Where," asks this writer, "is that spirit of self-sacrifice and devotion to be found today?" Alas, purblind ignorance! Alas for prejudice which will not see! Alas for the deafness which cannot hear and the stupidity which will, being whole, not understand!

And so you see my philanthropic work, such as it has been, has been due entirely to two or three novels. I drew a picture as faithfully as I could and I was identified with the picture. People supposed that because I had drawn with a certain amount of understanding my heart was full of sympathy. The calls upon me went far to create that sympathy. First I drew what I saw; then my sympathy went out towards my models; the next step was to write for them, to work for them, to speak for them. But I began to speak late in life. I have never been a speaker; I lacked the small things of the orator—the current common phrase with which he effects the *junctura callida* of various divisions. Moreover, I had a difficulty to manage my voice; when I grew excited, when I felt my audience with me, I was carried away, I spoke too fast. Yet there were occasions on which I could, and did, speak effectively— notably one occasion at the Mansion House when I certified to what I knew and had proved concerning the social work of the Salvation Army.

I shall not, I suppose, speak much more in public. I can only hope that in my various addresses I may have done good, if only to dispel some prejudice; that I may have induced some of the younger and more generous spirits to take upon them, whether for the Salvation Army or someother cause, that spirit of self-sacrifice, of devotion, of voluntary obscurity which, *pace* the *Spectator* is in this generation awake and alive among us and is working marvels.

XIV*

The Survey of London

In October 1894 I began the survey of London, having entered into an arrangement with Messrs. A. & C. Black, the publishers of the *Encyclopædia Britannica*, for its production.

The survey of London was first undertaken by John Stow, and the first edition was published in 1598. His work remains as the basis of all following works on the same subject. It is indeed remarkable to observe how very little was added to Stow for a long time. Anthony Munday, James Howell, and a "Society of Gentlemen" successively brought out new editions of Stow's *Survey*—not always under that name—during the seventeenth century. In 1720 an edition brought up to date with maps and excellent illustrations was issued by John Strype in two volumes folio. This was followed by *The Circuit Walk*, or *Perambulation*. In 1754 another edition of Stow and Strype appeared with very little alteration. In the same year William Maitland produced his *History and Survey of London* which was original and, for the time, very good. Other books came out on the history of London with or without the *Perambulation*. These, whether they bore the name of Lambert, Allen, or Entick, were practically copies of Maitland—mere copies verbatim of page after page. Harrison's history, which belongs to the same time as Maitland, is also for the most part a copy. Since the appearance of Strype—that is to say for nearly a hundred and fifty years—there has been no survey of London. Maps of London there are, books on various points connected with London—such as the history of a suburb, of a church, of an institution—but there has been no survey.

My proposal was to conduct such a survey. The plan was as follows: First, the history of London from the earliest times to the end of the nineteenth century was to be written by myself. I have now (1901) completed the work down to the end of the eighteenth century. This history includes the rise and growth of the government of London,

---

* This chapter gives only an outline of the author's design; but Sir Walter Besant intended to make additions to it, and also to allude here in detail to his several books on London. Moreover he hoped that the *Survey* would see the light during his life, when the work would speak for itself.

the story of its religious houses, the daily life of the people, the records of trade, shipping, buildings—everything that can be found for a reconstruction and restoration of the City from age to age. The history of Westminster and of Limehouse was planned to follow the history of the City. The antiquities of London and of its ancient suburbs were to be detailed after this. The City churches were to be described with their chantries and monuments. There were to be monographs on St. Paul's, Westminster Abbey, the Inns of Court, the Tower of London, and other important places. The perambulations of the City and its suburbs, including the whole area covered by the London County Council, were to come next. We were then to give the history of London as it is today, with all its buildings and institutions, including a history of education in London from the earliest times to the end of the nineteenth century.

This was the task that lay before me. I began with the perambulations, which were carried out for me by three or four active and intelligent young people. For my own part I set to work at once upon the history. I confess that had I known the enormity of the labours before me, I should not have undertaken the work. Everyone will understand that the number of points constantly cropping up and demanding investigation could not be estimated beforehand. My original design was to give the whole day to the work except when I had fiction in hand—that is to say, to give about eight months of the year. When I was working upon a novel I gave up my mornings from nine to twelve to fiction; and my afternoons—from half-past one till six—to the Survey. A change of work does not fatigue one so much as continuing steadily at the same work. To put away the fiction, which I did at home, and to take up the Survey, which I wrote in town, was a refreshing change, the work being divided by the time taken up in getting into town. However, when I look at the masses of typewritten material which represent the six years of work at the Survey, I am astonished that I have been able to carry out so much with my own hand. I resolved, at the outset, to undertake the history alone, but I found it necessary to take over a great deal more. I mention the Survey as part—a good part—of my life's work. I know not how it will be received. There is so vast a field to be covered. The modern discoveries made concerning mediaeval London and the recent publications of the Corporation have given me a quantity of material never before used or put together. I need not here furnish a list of these books: that will be found in the Survey itself. Let it only be remembered that I have been able to break away altogether from Maitland and to treat the City from new materials and newly published records.

I have only to say, further, on this point, that I hope to see the publication begun this year (1901), and that I am, further, in hopes that the history and the Survey will be found worthy of the time and the subject. The beginning of the twentieth century is a fitting time for such a Survey to appear, and it is interesting to think that it is as nearly as possible three hundred years since the first edition of Stow was published.

XV

The Atlantic Union

I n my belief and according to my experience, if anything is to be accomplished it must be by the initiative of one man. A society with the full machinery of president, vice-president, and committee may be created, but then, when all is told, the work will be the work of one man, who must think for the society, live for it, act for it, and give all his time to it. The man who does the work need not be the man who started it.

One of the last associations with the start of which I was associated—though one of which I beg to state I was never the mainspring or the thinking machine—was the Atlantic Union.

The origin and the meaning of the Society was as follows:—

I observed when I last visited the United States in 1893, a blind and stupid hostility to England, partly made up of prejudice and ignorance, and partly due to the press of New York, which caters in great measure for the Irish, and is copied by the country papers without asking what motives have actuated the misrepresentation of things English. In illustration of this hostility I observed that the attitude of almost everybody in America towards England was then one of suspicion; whatever was done by this country was regarded and treated at the outset as presumably done with an evil motive or with unworthy considerations. I observed further, that the individual Englishman was received with friendliness and kindness; that he can reckon on friendliness. Also that there exists, all over the States, a great deal of interest in everything that concerns the old country; in news and telegrams from England, in our literature, in our views of things. I saw also that the ignorance of our institutions in the States is simply amazing. We talk about the laws being the same; the foundation of the law is the same, but there are enormous differences. For instance, no Americans seem able to understand loyalty; our personal respect and affection for the sovereign is to *them* incomprehensible; they do not understand the restrictions of sovereignty, and expect from the sovereign the same personal and irresponsible acts and words as from an ordinary person. Again, as to the House of Lords, their ignorance and prejudice are colossal. Mostly they think that it comprises all the sons as well as the holders of the title; and they are fully convinced that a noble lord is and must be a profligate and *roué*. If you ask them why, they point probably to some noble lord who has been figuring in the States with a variety actress, leaving his wife at home; or to some scandal in which someother noble lord or some younger son with a courtesy title is concerned. That the House of Lords consists almost entirely of elderly and quite respectable gentlemen, many of whom have received or succeeded to their titles late in life; who are not too rich; who are for the most part interested in local, rather than in national matters; who are chairmen of county institutions and supporters of the agricultural interest; who leave their legislative functions to the care of a dozen or twenty statesmen and as many lawyers—that such is our House of Lords is a thing that they cannot believe, and will not believe, because it conflicts with one of their most cherished prejudices. Indeed this prejudice I have found among Americans who have been here over and over again. Now, one is not called upon to defend either the limited monarchy or the Upper House to Americans; but it would certainly be well if they could learn at least the facts of the case. As it is, they are unable to understand the existence of free institutions, and personal liberty of thought, speech, and action, together with (1) a sovereign whose power—but this, again, they cannot understand—is far less than that of their President; and (2) a House of Lords not elected by the people, whose modest functions are to put on the drag, to prevent the passing of ill-considered measures, and to allow no great or important step to be taken until they are well assured that it is the will of the people.

Again, consider the attitude of the average American towards the Anglican Church. I suppose that the Episcopal Church in the States does regard the Anglican branch with respect or with appreciation. But the average American does not belong to the Episcopal Church. I have found in the average American a rooted belief (1) that our clergy are enormously rich; (2) that they do nothing; (3) that such a thing as piety is not known to them; (4) that the patronage of the Church is in the hands of "the aristocracy," who put their younger sons into all the enviable berths. These prejudices are kept alive by an ill-informed or malignant press in America; by certain dissenting ministers in this country whose hatred of the Church has a social origin—let us own that of late the appearance of scholars and divines among the Nonconformist ministers is changing the social aspect of the case; and by the traditions of persecution which still linger in the memory of the New England folk. The prejudices can be answered only by reference to figures and to facts which cannot be disputed. The poverty of the English clergy is far greater than the poverty of the American ministers; the number of good livings in England is much less than the number of well-paid churches in New England. The Anglican bishops, whose incomes appear large, cannot, as a rule, save much from what they receive. They are, for the most part, elderly when they are appointed; they have to keep up open house all the year round; they have to support every kind of charitable and religious enterprise; they are always contributing to the support of poor clergy, of clergymen's widows and orphans, and schools and so on; they travel about, and are always obliged to keep up a staff of chaplains and secretaries. The bishop is paid for the maintenance and leadership of the diocese and all that his diocese means; he is the figure-head, the chairman, the advocate; without a bishop the diocese falls to pieces. As regards piety, what need be said when we can point to the long and glorious history of the English Church—to the names of Ken, Hooker, Herbert, Heber, or, in later times, Keble, Pusey, Maurice, Robertson, Stanley and hundreds of others less known to fame? As to the patronage of the Church, one has only to look into the *Clergy List* to find out what that is worth and how it is bestowed.

An American once wrote to me giving me, with a great air of triumph, what he was pleased to consider a damning fact for the Church—viz., that the patron of a certain benefice had actually bestowed it upon his illegitimate son first and then upon that holder's son. He did not explain why illegitimacy should make a man unfit for Holy Orders or for holding a living; nor did he explain how it was that the bishop had accepted for the benefice a man unfit, as my American evidently considered the man to be. But then he was quite ignorant that the bishop had anything to do with the appointment.

These prejudices are not, of course, so strong with the educated and the cultured Americans as with the average American; still, they do exist, more or less, with nearly all. They are difficult to be cleared away because they assist the American in that feeling of superiority which is dear to every nationality. It is perhaps dearer to an American than to a Frenchman or a German; and I think that one of the causes of the American hostility to England that I noticed during my stay in the United States in 1893 is that we do not recognise that superiority. We do not, in fact, care in the least whether a foreign country thinks itself superior to ourselves or not. But we do see that the American claim is partly based on ignorance and prejudice. And we should be very pleased if we could, by any means in our power, remove some of that prejudice.

I next observed that a great number of Americans—and, for that matter, of people from our own large colonies—come to this country every year; that they stay a short time in London; that they travel about England to a certain extent, seeing cathedrals, castles, churches, and historic places; that they bring with them no letters of introduction; that they never enter an English house or make a friend of any English man or woman; that they see everything from the outside only; and that they go away again with all their prejudice and ignorance as strong as ever. For you see, you cannot master the history, or understand the present condition, of the Church of England by standing in a village churchyard or by looking through a cathedral.

This is a long preamble. It leads up to the creation of the Atlantic Union.

The Society admits as members Englishmen, Irishmen and Scotchmen, Australians, Canadians, citizens of any British colony, and Americans. Because the Canadians and the citizens of the United States represent the largest field, it is called the Atlantic Union. We want to see branches in all the great cities, which shall offer some kind of hospitality to members of other branches. For instance, we in London engage ourselves to receive Americans and others, to show them collective and individual attention; we organise for them personally conducted walks and visits; we shall be able to let them see more than is shown to the average stranger; we shall hold receptions; we shall get up dinners, concerts, lectures; certain ladies will give garden-parties and "at-homes"; we shall make up parties to go to Oxford and Cambridge and to certain cathedrals and other places; and during the whole time we shall endeavour to present our own institutions as they are—without comparisons: *as they are*.

Again, we shall not attempt to get hold of millionaires, nor can we offer our friends an opening into "London Society." We want to attract the classes which have most influence in the colonies and in the States—the professional classes, lawyers, physicians, authors, teachers. And on our side we shall offer the society of the corresponding classes—of cultivated and educated people, men and women of science, followers of art, literature, journalism, and the learned professions generally. It is a great scheme; it is now (1901) only in its second year; but I think—I hope—that it has a future before it.

XVI

Conclusion: The Conduct of Life and the Influence of Religion

I am writing in the decline of life, when the sixtieth birthday is already five years behind, and one must contemplate the possibility of immediate dissolution and the certainty of a speedy end; when all that life has to give, or that fortune chooses to give, has been already given. The love of woman; of wife and children; the allotted measure of success; the joy of work; the joy of struggle; the joy of victory; the love of friends who have gone before and of friends who are left; the reputation, whatever it may be—all these things have been received and enjoyed; and with them the piled-up hatreds and revenges of the baser sort. There is work still to be done: it is the carrying on of old work, not the making of new work. We gather up the threads and accomplish the task, happy if it has been a task so weighty as to be prolonged into the year three score and ten.

Let me end these reminiscences with a few words befitting the close of a life—being upon the Conduct of Life and the Influence of Religion.

One is not expected to be much above the standards of one's own time. At school, for instance, we had no athletics to speak of in my time; we played cricket and football, we ran races. There was no responsibility laid upon the back of the senior boys yet; in a way they did look after the juniors—it was an irresponsible and spontaneous fashion; such words as "good form" and "bad form" were unknown, yet the things were known.

At King's College, London, the professors and lecturers took no personal interest in the students; the principal. Dr. Jelf, knew nothing of them and paid them no attention; nobody cared whether they read; nobody ever considered it worth while to look after the better sort; we were all left absolutely alone. There was no college life in the place, no clubs, no social intercourse among the students. The idea was simply to present the means of learning if the men chose to avail themselves of the gift; in the same way the old and still lingering administration of the Church was to open the doors, to present the means of grace, and to allow those who wished to avail themselves of the gift. Outside the college, I have already explained, I used to wander about the City. But there was the evening to get through. No one appeared to know how desperately miserable an evening all alone in lodgings may be. I have sat with my books before me while the silence grew more and more intolerable, rising up all round as a cloud hiding the rest of the world. When my nerves would stand it no longer, I have taken my hat and rushed out into the streets.

The evening amusements of London were more varied, and far, far more coarse than they are now. As a young fellow of eighteen I ought not to have gone to them—that is quite certain. Yet what could be done when solitude became intolerable? There were the theatres at half-price—there were not many theatres, and in a week or two one could get through them all. There were the dancing places of the more decorous sort, the Argyle Rooms, the Holborn Casino, "Caldwell's," besides places whose reputation was such that one was afraid to venture within their walls. At the Holborn and the Argyle the ladies were very beautifully dressed. I did not go there to dance or to make their acquaintance; I sat on the red velvet benches and listened to the music. At "Caldwell's," on the other hand, where the girls were more simply attired, and where they liked to meet a young fellow who could dance, and could dance tolerably well, I did dance. Perhaps it was wrong; perhaps, however, it was not. I take no blame to myself on account of "Caldwell's."

There were places not quite so Innocent whither my wandering footsteps led me. There were the Coal Hole, the Cider Cellars, Evans's. At these places there was singing; some of the songs were very beautiful and very well sung; part songs were given at Evans's; *poses plastiques* were offered for the corruption of youth at a place whose name I have forgotten; and at the Coal Hole or the Cider Cellars there was "Baron" Nicholson and the "judge and jury." Such an exhibition would not be tolerated at the present day; I remember it as clever but inconceivably coarse. In the summer one could go to Cremorne or to Highbury Barn; even, for curiosity, walk to the Eagle in the City Road. When I remember all these places and how, in order to escape the awful stillness of my lodgings, I would go out in the evening and prowl about looking in here and there, I wonder that some horrible obsession of the devil did not fall upon me, as it fell upon hundreds and thousands of young fellows like myself, turned into the streets because I could not bear to sit alone. Why, there were clerks and students all round me; every house in my street was filled with them; every man sat in his own dismal cell and listened to the silence till his nerves could stand it no longer. Then he went out into the street. If there are fifty devils in the streets today, there were five hundred then. It was not everyone who at eighteen was so boyish in mind and manner and in appearance as I was; not everyone who was short-sighted and shy; not everyone who was able to sit among the rabble rout and listen to the music as if surrounded by nymphs and swains of the highest purity and virtue.

However, the thing to be remembered is that London was much coarser in its evening amusements then than now; that the outward show of morals was not insisted upon so much. London is bad enough now, but in most localities only after ten o'clock and before twelve, whereas in the fifties things went on all day long. I remember that among the houses south of Waterloo Bridge there was a whole row where in the ground floor windows there was everyday an exhibition of girls dancing up and down, and inviting the young men to come in. And I remember that, apart from the "judge and jury" business, the songs sung at some places were coarse beyond belief. And considering all these things, I cannot wonder that I went to them, having no one to warn or to restrain me, or to offer any substitutes for the amusements which were gross enough, yet promised the attractions of music and singing.

At Cambridge there were none of these things. Yet there were coarsenesses at Cambridge which one looks back upon with surprise. After dinner (the dinner hour was four—an unholy hour) there were "wines" which were often prolonged far into the evening. There were also suppers, and at wines and at suppers men sang songs which would not now be tolerated by the most rowdy set in the most rowdy college. Then there was little or no disguise if a man supported the suburb called Barnwell; the only thing was that he must not be caught by the proctors. The suburb was well populated and freely discussed. That a man was intended for Holy Orders did not offer an obstacle to this patronage of Barnwell; there were fellows of colleges who were as bad as the undergraduates in this respect. I mention the fact simply to show the temptations to which young men were then exposed. Nothing is more remarkable than the change at my university in respect to wine—and Barnwell. Meantime it must not be supposed that there were no undergraduates of a higher tone or a purer life; on the contrary, there were many; their lives, their conversation, their habits were a continual protest against the general low level.

In a word, the youth of my time were brought up in the midst of great laxity of morals, great coarseness of conversation, amusements gross and unseemly, yet with the existence all around them of Puritan austerity and the condemnation of the reasonable recreations of life. Unfortunately the Puritan austerity demanded too much of young men; it could only be adopted by the few who were as cold-blooded as fishes, or by the fanatics who curbed themselves with resolution and by violence. For it condemned all amusements. "Could you," said one, and it was thought by his following to be a clincher—"could you say grace before sitting down to cards." The answer would be now "Of course— why not?" For indeed there is no reason why, if we are not Pharisaic, we should not thank God for every innocent recreation. "Can you," asked another, "put your arm round the waist of a girl in the dance without thoughts of love?" The answer is now obvious. Formerly it was not so obvious. "Can you," asked a third austerely, "go to the theatre while your immortal soul remains to be saved?" And so they went on. Is there any wonder that the revolt against the Evangelicals waited only for the spark, and that when this spark was applied by the newly founded *Saturday Review* the defeat and the rout of the Evangelicals speedily followed.

The Evangelicals represented for the most part a pitiless and horrible Calvinism, The world groaned under the dreadful creed. Not only did it limit the mercy of God and the mediation of Christ to an insignificant minority, but it held that as a man died—at the moment of death—so his soul was affected forever. I remember how a cousin of mine was drowned when I was a boy. The young fellow had told his mother that he was not going to the water; he changed his mind and went; and he was drowned. The kindly religious folk said that he had gone to meet his God with a lie upon his lips, and that his doom was certain. You may imagine the agony and misery of his mother.

For my own part I began to read the works of Frederick Denison Maurice; he taught me the way out of the Evangelical creed and I followed that way with the greatest alacrity.

Having shovelled away the Evangelical rubbish, I was ready to make a clean sweep of a good deal more. I do not suppose that anyone wants to know how I arrived at my present simple creed, but such as it is, perhaps it may interest some readers:—

I believe, in an intelligent Mind who hears, listens, guides, and directs; to which nothing is small, nothing is mean, nothing is contemptible;

which leads a Darwin in the direction of discovery, or grants what is good for a simple girl; which has ordered the evolution of an insect as much as that of a man.

I believe that this Mind has in some way ordered the conversion of a ball of flaming rock into a globe covered with vegetation. In other words, what we call the laws of Nature are due to the Mind. They are laws to which all life is subject; if they are broken, the breaker suffers.

I believe that these laws are in a moral or spiritual order as well as physical order. The discovery of this moral order has been made little by little, but the greatest contributors to the discovery have been the Jewish prophets, ending with Jesus.

If one calls him the Son of God, why not? We are all the Sons of God, and He is the greatest. That He was martyred was a natural result of His teaching at such a time.

The doctrine of atonement by blood is found in every age and in every country; it forms a part of the great theory of sacrifice—viz., the propitiation of the Deity, as a Deity, by something rare and precious as the eldest son, or a captive, or so many head of cattle or of sheep. We no longer believe in the sacrifice and altars, in giving roast beef to the Lord, or in offering him streams of wine or human sacrifices. We no longer believe in blood being poured out in order to propitiate the Deity. Therefore to speak of the blood of Jesus is a mere survival in words of an exploded belief.

The pretensions of the so-called Christian priest are not more foolish than the pretensions of any other priest. The Jewish prophets have proclaimed, in words that ought to serve once for all, their contempt for the Jewish priest. The spirit of sacerdotalism is the same in every religion and in every age. The priest claims supernatural powers; we convert bread into flesh and wine into blood; we confer some mysterious benefit by baptising the child, marrying the man and woman, and burying them. The priest surrounds himself with mystery, gets inside a sacred enclosure, mumbles, makes signs, puts on vestments. He does this whether he is making taboo in a Polynesian island, or mumbo-jumbo in West Africa, or obeah in Jamaica, or is a Roman Catholic priest in St. Peter's or a Ritualist in an English church.

Meantime foolish people—whose folly is boundless and amazing and past all understanding—spend their lives in fighting over what is, or is not, allowed in this or that Prayer Book. Not content with the slavery of the letter of the Bible, they have become slaves of the letter of the Prayer Book. Now, set the Prayer Book aside and appeal to common sense and experience.

Experience, at least, yells and shouts in our ears, only we will not understand, the fact that auricular confession is a slavery; that it destroys the will and that it leads a man to surrender his judgment and his freedom of action, and makes him in the conduct of life little better than a child.

The reservation of the host is proved to be fertile in superstition, in charges of blasphemy, and in the extension of priestly domination. The only excuse for it is that a man may die before the bread can be consecrated—as if it mattered in such a case, or in any case, whether the bread was consecrated or not.

The use of incense was originally introduced to correct the atmosphere during a crowded service in hot countries. If it were not, can anyone not corrupted by the ecclesiastical rubbish believe that the Lord is pleased by creating a stink in a church?

Some of the poor fanatics are desirous of introducing prayers for the dead; can they possibly be ignorant of the fact that the system means prayers for those who can pay, and the creation of chanting priests, to sing services—propitiatory services—for those who can pay? And can they see any difference between such a service, mumbled as a daily duty by a priest paid for the duty, and the mechanical prayers of a Buddhist priest? And can they reconcile this senseless repetition with any mercy, however inadequate, of an intelligent Creator and Father?

In fine, the more I consider the question—and it has been forced upon my consideration more than upon that of many men—the more I understand that the whole of the ecclesiastical system, with the pretensions of the clergy, the mock mystery of their ritual, the supernatural nonsense of their claims, their schemes for the domination of the human intellect, their ecclesiastical trappings, mouthings, murmurings, confessings, incense, consecration rites, and all the rest of it, are foolish, baseless, and to the highest degree mischievous.

Christianity seems to me a perfectly simple religion; it consists not only in a blameless life, but in a life whose ideals are continually growing higher and more noble. That this is possible, is in itself to me a proof of another life to follow this.

In Christianity I find no place for priest or for mysteries of man's own making. The world is full of mysteries; all life is a mystery never to be discovered. There is the great and wonderful mystery of birth—can anything be more mysterious or more wonderful. There is the mystery of growth, the mystery of manhood and of strength, the mystery of decay and death. Why do we decay at sixty and die at seventy? There are the mysteries of disease, there are the mysteries of man's intellectual achievements, his scientific discoveries, his subjugation of natural forces, his invention, his music and his arts, his poetry, in which he seems to draw back the veil—he only dreams of drawing it back, but he magnetises his audience so that for a time they think that they are looking at the things behind. Good Heavens! These are the great and solemn mysteries. To consider them, to work upon them, showing their reality since we can never show their cause, to study them, to make discoveries in them—these are things worthy of man, worthy of true religion. Why invent sham and meaningless mysteries which are but words, which lead to nothing but the mischievous intervention between God and man of a fellow-man who pretends to useless powers and professes to hold the keys of heaven?

A blameless life—what is it? You will find it all in the Sermon on the Mount, if you are wise enough to understand what is meant, and not to interpret it by the letter.

And so I leave my belief and my life. Looking back, as I have done in these chapters, I remember a good many mistakes—somethings even which I should be ashamed to set down in this page. But the book is not one of confessions. I could not pretend, as regards the things not set down, to be repentant; if I were to sprinkle ashes over my head, it would be, perhaps, while I was recalling the thing itself with a lingering pleasure. I have shown you the conditions of my early manhood; the finish of those conditions may be guessed, as much as you please. And as to my religious views, they have gradually come to me. Little by little they have formed themselves in my mind until they have become part and parcel of me. Now at last there is not left to me a single rag or scrap of the ecclesiastical rubbish. I do not seek to convert any of my readers to my own views; only, my very dear friends, if you could understand the freedom—the happy freedom—of the soul, when you have succeeded in recognising the utter baselessness of the priestly pretensions, you would at least take the trouble to find out what the views mean.

A Note About the Author

Walter Besant (1836–1901) was an English novelist and historian. Born at Portsmouth, Hampshire, Besant was the son of a wine merchant, whose other children included William, a prominent mathematician, and Frank, the husband of renowned theosophist, socialist, and activist Annie Besant. After attending King's College London, he enrolled at Christ's College, Cambridge to study mathematics, graduating with first class honors in 1859. Besant worked for six years as professor of mathematics at Royal College, Mauritius, returning to London in 1867 after a period of ill-health. In 1868, he published his work *Studies in French Poetry* and was appointed to the Palestine Exploration Fund as Secretary. Three years later, Besant was called to the bar at Lincoln's Inn and began his literary collaboration with novelist James Rice. Together, they wrote such successful works of fiction as *Ready-money Mortiboy* (1872) and *The Golden Butterfly* (1876).

A Note from the Publisher

Spanning many genres, from non-fiction essays to literature classics to children's books and lyric poetry, Mint Edition books showcase the master works of our time in a modern new package. The text is freshly typeset, is clean and easy to read, and features a new note about the author in each volume. Many books also include exclusive new introductory material. Every book boasts a striking new cover, which makes it as appropriate for collecting as it is for gift giving. Mint Edition books are only printed when a reader orders them, so natural resources are not wasted. We're proud that our books are never manufactured in excess and exist only in the exact quantity they need to be read and enjoyed.

Discover more of your favorite classics with Bookfinity™.

- Track your reading with custom book lists.
- Get great book recommendations for your personalized Reader Type.
- Add reviews for your favorite books.
- AND MUCH MORE!

Visit **bookfinity.com** and take the fun Reader Type quiz to get started.

Enjoy our classic and modern companion pairings!

Classic & Modern